T0327835

IN THEIR DEFENCE

IN THEIR DEFENCE

Fighting for Youth Justice
ONE CHILD AT A TIME

AIKA STEPHENSON
and EMMA DONNAN

Michael O'Mara Books Limited

First published in Great Britain in 2024 by
Michael O'Mara Books Limited
9 Lion Yard
Tremadoc Road
London SW4 7NQ

A CIP catalogue record for this book is available from the British Library.

The author and publishers have endeavoured to verify all the facts and
statistics in this book with bona fide sources. Neither the author nor the
publisher can guarantee the accuracy or usability of any information
contained herein, nor accept any liability for any injury or loss that may
occur as a result of information given in this book. Some names and
identifying details have been changed to protect the privacy of individuals.

This product is made of material from well-managed, FSC®-certified
forests and other controlled sources. The manufacturing processes
conform to the environmental regulations of the country of origin.

ISBN: 978-1-78929-487-3 in hardback print format
ISBN: 978-1-78929-489-7 in ebook format

1 2 3 4 5 6 7 8 9 10

Cover design by Ana Bjezancevic
Designed and typeset by Barbara Ward
Printed and bound by CPI Group (UK) Ltd, Croydon, CR0 4YY

www.mombooks.com

CONTENTS

Foreword   6

Introduction – A Journey into Law   9

1   The Police Interview – It's Just an Honest Conversation, Right?   17

2   Up in Court   45

3   How Schools are Letting Our Children Down   71

4   Choose Your Friends Carefully   95

5   Social Media, Sex and the Law   111

6   Another Pandemic – County Drug Lines   127

7   When Children's Homes Go Wrong   145

8   Neurodiversity, Mental Health and the Law   155

9   Is the Legal System Racist?   177

10   Is a Seventeen-Year-Old an Adult or a Child?   209

11   Crown Court   217

12   Different Sentencing Options   243

Afterword: Fuelled by Hope   255

Acknowledgements   261

Contacts   265

Index   266

Foreword

- Can my ten-year-old really be arrested for causing a playground tumble?

- Why would anyone get caught up in county drug lines?

- Is the law tougher on black teenage boys?

- Do the police need to tell me if my seventeen-year-old is arrested?

- Why are there suddenly police officers in so many schools?

No expectant parent envisages their son or daughter's childhood being tainted by arrest or conviction. That only happens to other people's 'naughty kids', right? Wrong.

After years of working with young people involved in the criminal justice system, I have seen how the law impacts the lives of every young person, from the obviously vulnerable, to the A-grade student from a traditionally stable upbringing. Every parent has questions like those above, but in reality there is very little information out there, and it is time we all knew the answers.

No child is ever immune to being caught up in the law, whether as a defendant, witness, or victim, so being armed with knowledge ahead of time is a clear advantage.

I am a solicitor and expert in youth justice with Just for Kids Law (JfKL), a not-for-profit organization, and I spend my days tackling misinformation and miscarriages of justice, and trying to ensure that every child has access to fair treatment within the legal system. Every day in my job is about giving young people a voice, fair treatment, and a hopeful future. My work gives me highs and lows – it is heartbreaking at times, and at others, fills me with joy.

I want to tell you about the extraordinary cases that make up my daily life, and lay bare what really goes on behind the scenes, from the police station through to the young offender institution, and everything in between. The list of changes I dream of making in the youth justice system goes on for miles, but for now, the less there is a shroud of mystery over it, and the more informed we all are, the better protected our children will be.

INTRODUCTION

A Journey into Law

Lots of children decide what they want to be when they grow up based on encouragement from their parents, or a fleeting event that may seem insignificant to an adult, but leaves an impression. They had a nice doctor when they broke their arm, so they want to go into medicine. Those flashing fire-engines caught their eye, so they want to be a firefighter.

In my case, visiting my dad in prison when I was ten years old was the moment that changed the course of my life, and influenced the career choices I was to make. I didn't fully understand what was going on, but I knew I wanted to be the person who could get him out of there.

My childhood wasn't one you might envisage for a future lawyer. But I find stereotyping is generally detrimental to young people and society as a whole – as you will see throughout this book – so as you read it I'd ask you to leave your own preconceived ideas behind too.

My dad grew up in Jamaica, one of five children. When he was a teenager his parents came to the UK as part of the Windrush generation. My gran found work as a domestic help in a hospital and Granddad took on hours in a factory, while Dad helped look after the rest of the children back in Jamaica, until they gradually moved over to the UK to join their parents, a couple at a time. It meant school wasn't really an option for him, and he always struggled to read and write, so with very few job opportunities open to him once he arrived over here, it was inevitable that he became a bit of a hustler to get by.

Meanwhile my mum, a white British girl, was living a sheltered upbringing on a farm in Bedfordshire. From day one though, she had bigger dreams, with plans to escape to a city, and clear ideas on justice and civil rights and how she could help save the world. She met my dad, and, by the time she was seventeen, she had given birth to my sister; at nineteen, she had me. But my parents' relationship was a volatile one, and as quickly as their worlds collided, things imploded and it fell apart.

The next few years for my sister and I were spent between a farm in Somerset with my mum and her parents, and with my dad at his home in Luton.

It was when I was seven, that Dad first went to prison. I can't remember the reason, but it was to be the start of a period of his life when he was in and out of jail.

I developed a negative view of the police from a young age, watching the interactions when my dad was stopped when we were out and about, and learning to be alert to police cars, pointing them out to my dad. We would visit him in prison, and while I didn't fully understand it, I knew he was being kept there against his will, and I didn't like it. I wanted him at home with me and these police and prison guards were the people who were stopping that. So at ten, when I began to get a basic understanding of the role played by lawyers in all of this, I decided that was what I was going to be.

The following years were spent between parents' and grandparents' homes. My number of siblings was growing, until I had seven brothers and sisters with us all sharing the same dad, but having five mums between us.

When I was eleven, my older sister and I moved into a three-bed, semi-detached house in Luton with my gran – my dad's mum. It was a typical West Indian household, strict and old-fashioned, but filled with love. I would share a bed with my gran (my granddad had died by then), while my sister slept with my aunty, and my uncle was in a box room. My gran worked so hard and was so kind to everyone; she would come home from the hospital armed with flowers and thank you cards from grateful staff and patients. She was – and still is – a massive factor in bringing stability to my life, and is really important to me.

One day, when I was fifteen and my sister and I were back living with dad, I came home from school to find the police arresting him in the street, and the house being searched. That feeling of standing helplessly in my bedroom, while our belongings were turned upside down around me, and looking out the window to see my dad in handcuffs, will stay with me forever. I was angry, sad, confused, and feeling incredibly violated.

This time he was sentenced to three years in prison.

I was a studious teen, and turned my focus to my GCSEs. Books had always been my escape from the trauma and madness of life. Someone could be having a full-blown fight in front of me, but I would be completely tuned in to the world in my book.

My sister was living quite a wild life – reacting I think in her own way to our childhood. At the same time, we had several friends who were in care, and others who were going through a hard time. Our house became a go-to place for anyone who wasn't getting on with family, or who needed somewhere to stay just for a cooling-off period, or to get themselves together. We found ourselves trying to help people out, taking in the chaos that was around us, and giving it some shape and direction.

There is no doubt that I had seen far too much at too young an age, and I probably was mentally older than many of my peers. But it was an important time in informing the way I now work, as I can look back at my fifteen-year-old self and see both the capabilities and vulnerabilities that are possible at that age.

Making use of my grade success, I headed to college, then my mum and stepdad paid for me to go to law school. I had the idea that I might focus on the areas of child abduction, or family law.

After graduating, my first job was in a corporate law firm, and the attitude from everyone in the business was, 'This was it: I have made it', because it was a 'magic circle firm' (i.e. one of the top five in London for prestige and profitability). I hadn't been a fully A-grade student – my degree was a 2:2 – so I would never have got a training contract, but I found my way in by taking a role as a paralegal, with the idea that I would work my way up. It quickly became clear that any ideas I had of a glamorous life now I was away from student life and in the real legal world, were unfounded. The reality was, I was spending days indexing documents and was bored out of my mind. This was not what I had imagined for myself at all.

My aunt worked at Feltham Young Offender Institution (YOI) and told me about a job that had come up there as an advocate for children who had been remanded in custody. It might not have been my dream job in terms of making use of all my studies, but it at least sounded like I would have responsibilities and challenges, and I could make a difference to the experiences of these children. I applied and was offered the job on the basis of both my qualifications and my background – they believed I stood a better chance of relating to these children than most in the profession, perhaps something that has been true throughout my career.

My role was to find out why each young person was there, work out which local authority they came under, speak to the different services, assess what was viable, and put together a package to show if and how a child could safely be released on bail while awaiting trial. It was about looking at the bigger picture for the accused and the victim and seeing if there was a way we could safely avoid custody for the former, until a case proceeded or was dropped. So, for example, if an incident had happened in or close to a child's home and they couldn't go back there, were there other options? Were there different places they could stay, such as with other family or friends? It was effectively a welfare role, where I was their connection to the outside world, and doing my best to get them back out there safely.

Inevitably, it wasn't a nine-to-five job that allowed me to go home in the evening and switch off. I'd leave at the end of the day with my little kit of belt, keys, and old-fashioned police station whistle – I was meant to blow it if I was in trouble but never did – and walking out of the gates I'd feel like I had been in prison myself. I could never put the children from that day out of my head, even once I was home, and would often spend nights pondering if there were other ways to help them.

One thing that shocked me from the off, was just how quickly being in prison could change a young person, by which I mean I could literally see a transformation within hours.

Children would arrive crying, vulnerable, unsupported, perhaps without their parents even knowing they were there. They would be scared, and at times feeling suicidal as I and other staff dealt with their initial paperwork.

Then, forty-eight hours later, if they were still at the institute, I might see them in the corridor, pausing to give me a nod, 'Y'alright, miss?' The vulnerability they displayed in our last meeting was now completely gone, hidden behind an emotionless mask. It was shocking how quickly they seemed to adapt and harden their minds to these new surroundings. Children rapidly learned what they needed to do to survive in there, and disconnecting their actions from their feelings was unfortunately a key skill.

It really felt that in a lot of cases, by sending children to prison, we were teaching them how to detach themselves, and compartmentalize actions and emotions. I was worried that once they learned this was a way to survive in life, it was going to be hard to undo that back in the outside world. Disconnecting actions and emotions from each other at such an early age is highly problematic. It means a person can commit a crime and not really feel anything for the victim. Was a removal of empathy really what we wanted to instil in our young people in prison?

Soon, I was beginning to wonder who was actually benefiting from them being locked up and seriously question whether any young person should ever face the prospect of prison. It was certainly clear it was doing nothing to make them more involved, positive and happy members of society.

I threw myself into the role, much more than was really required of me, and very quickly realized this was a life-changing job, that youth justice was my passion, and that I wanted to be a lawyer who practised and represented children in the criminal justice system. So I began applying for training contracts in the high street law firms that had the best reputations for social justice. I was put through psychometric testing, but it seemed either I wasn't the right personality profile, or my interview skills weren't up to scratch, as I kept getting rejections.

Instead I took a role as Bail and Remand Supervision Officer at Westminster Youth Offending Team, which was in a similar vein to my role at Feltham YOI. I was based at West London Magistrates' Court three days a week, so was able to put my legal knowledge to use, looking at bail options for children in the cells to avoid them being remanded in custody. On the other couple of days I was supervising young people on bail, looking at whichever area of their life was contributing to their offending, such as substance abuse, peer pressure, sexual exploitation, homelessness or poverty, and seeing how we could work towards changing those instigating factors for them.

Again, I loved the job, but I had two issues with it. Firstly, my mum kept saying to me: 'You went to law school to be a lawyer, so when are you going to do it?' Frustrating though her remarks were, I couldn't deny she had a point.

Then there was my irritation with a system that felt as if it was made up of lots of separate services created for young people, but none of them really interconnected. If I had to hear: 'That doesn't come under my remit' one more time! An adult might understand what falls under someone's job role, but for a child to be going to an adult, and trusting them with a problem, only to be told that helping on that front is not part of their job, can be very hard for that young person to understand. While the adult would often desperately like to help, but find themselves limited by bureaucracy, the child just hears, 'I'm not interested, you're on your own'.

Youth Offending Teams (YOTs) are multidisciplinary and meant to rectify this problem, but it still means young people with multiple needs having multiple appointments with multiple professionals. Really they just need one sole point of contact to help them out. It meant even really basic practical steps that would help a young person move forward, such as having a bank account or ID, weren't getting sorted out, as the child was passed from pillar to post.

Around this time I was the Youth Offending Team officer for a boy who was being represented by a barrister called Shauneen Lambe. She saw me arguing the case about his vulnerabilities with my manager, and realized I was a lot more invested than many of the other Youth Offending Team workers she had seen in action before.

Shauneen had been working on death penalty cases in New Orleans, and had just returned to the UK. She was trying to set up a specialist youth team at a local firm. As we chatted over a coffee we hit it off, and realized we had many of the same values, frustrations and ideas around the youth justice system. She suggested I take a training contract with her company, and we could combine our very different experiences towards reaching the same goal. It sounded perfect, so I did exactly as she suggested, and we began working towards this dream of a charitable legal firm, where we could tackle the bigger picture. By that I mean when a child had to go to court, we could offer legal representation, as well as real help to navigate through the legal system, and also a support network that might prevent them going down that route again. I would be a criminal solicitor, but with the more holistic approach that I had been so keen to see implemented. We also wanted to focus on fighting for reform on a wider level, using the evidence from our casework.

Within eighteen months, in 2006, Just for Kids Law was born. Since then it has grown and developed, taking on many more aims and arms, and we have had plenty of successes, as you will see – but there is still so much more to be done. Our biggest drive from the offset though has always been to give a voice to children and young people, something that has remained at the core of Just for Kids Law ever since.

CHAPTER 1

The Police Interview – It's Just an Honest Conversation, Right?

I am often asked if there is a common thread running through the lives of the children and young people we work with at Just for Kids Law, if a certain set of circumstances or a particular background is responsible for them ending up in the criminal justice system. I think those asking the question almost hope that there is, so that it can be packaged up and separated from the lives of their own child – 'Johnny will be fine, as that doesn't describe him at all.' It gives them a kind of safety net to view these children as 'others', removed from their own.

And the reality is, there are certainly conditions or situations that do increase a child's chance of arrest. These include, but are not limited to:

- Mental health issues
- Speech or language difficulties
- Living in care

- Being excluded from school
- Coming from a black or ethnic minority background
- Living in poverty or challenging situations

These are all influencing factors that we see on a regular basis in the lives of the children coming through the doors of Just for Kids Law.

Statistically it is also a sliding scale – the more of the above factors that a child is going through, the higher their chances of ending up in the criminal justice system. That is one of the saddest things about this for me: that the children who are already at a disadvantage before they have reached adulthood, who are struggling to find their place in the world, are the most likely to end up in a situation that will inevitably make their lives and their futures even tougher.

But as I said in the introduction, it is not by any means a cut-and-dried rule. Middle-class, monied, white, A-grade children from what would be seen as a traditionally stable background, can still come to the attention of the police. No one is immune. As a parent you can't just box off the 'bad kids', and assume that if your child doesn't tick any of those boxes, then you don't need to be clued up. Any child can find themselves in a legal nightmare that they or their parents had never imagined would be part of their lives.

The first contact I have with the majority of our clients is at the police station, when they are about to be interviewed for the first time. Often I will arrive with very little information about my client's situation, especially if I have been contacted by a panicked parent who is still in the dark themselves. Depending on the station and the time of day, it can be quiet and calm, or full of hustle and bustle, with people being booked in – some of them furious and shouting at the custody sergeant, others suffering the effect of withdrawing from drugs – while elsewhere are those in tears or standing quietly waiting in handcuffs.

It can be a disconcerting place for first-time visitors, but in my case, I am focused on just one thing – finding out all I can about the situation with my client before I meet them so that I can do my job to the best of my ability. How easy that will be quickly becomes apparent. Generally I'll be met by the officer on the case who will be doing the interview and who leads me through to the custody suite. I am sizing up the human aspect at this point and can get a good idea of whether they will be tricky from the outset by the way they talk about my client – if they make disparaging remarks, or are off-hand with me it obviously doesn't bode well. Often, if my client has been kept in custody for twelve hours before I was contacted, for no apparent reason, it can be a clear sign that we have different priorities in mind, and is probably a guarantee of hostility between us.

I am introduced to the custody sergeant who runs the suite and will give me access to the record. This gives a brief explanation of why my client has been arrested, as well as details of their time in custody: information such as whether they have eaten, slept, or been seen by a nurse. Then I go into a side room with the officer on the case, who should give me what is known as disclosure, the details around the arrest and possible charge. To give them their dues, sometimes the officer will be great and really open with the information. They are focused on the same thing as me: getting the interview and their job done, with no hidden agenda. However, with others it can be a very different matter. It can feel more like a game, where the officer thinks giving unhelpful, short or cryptic responses is clever, when in reality they are being obstructive to the legal process, and potentially damaging a child's future.

A rude or cocky officer might literally give me a one-line disclosure: 'He was arrested for assault', with no further information. That doesn't work for me – I want to know as many details as possible on what is understood to have happened, what exactly caused them to be arrested, and what the next steps might possibly be.

In court, the police can be criticized for not giving sufficient disclosure, as the aim is for me to be armed with enough information to be suitably equipped to advise my client appropriately. Simply knowing the charge does not put me in that situation. So if that one line is the extent of what I am given, I have to ask questions – Who is the alleged victim? Have you got a victim statement? Do you have CCTV? Are there witness statements? – partly as I can also be criticized at trial, but more importantly because I want to do right by my client.

At this point a police officer who withholds a lot of information, or is vague with it, suggests to me that they have a weak case and are trying to hide the fact they perhaps shouldn't have arrested my client at all. This is particularly common with cases such as affray, where officers regularly seem to pick up any young person in the area at the time of the incident, and work out who the genuine suspects are afterwards.

At times the officer can be obstructive to such a degree that I literally have to write 'Refused' next to every question I ask. This clash of conduct and purpose often surprises those not involved in law, as they assume we are all working together to find out the truth. Unfortunately I think this is one of the greatest misconceptions about the police.

Then, armed with whatever information I have managed to glean, it is time to meet the client. They will generally be a young person aged anything from ten to seventeen, and can be in any kind of emotional and mental state by this point. My initial role is to quickly assess how they are doing and react accordingly. They might be distressed, angry, exhausted, scared – I've faced every kind of emotion – and you can imagine how confusing and frightening it is, especially for those who have never been arrested before. This meeting takes place in a small interview room, where I explain my role and talk through what the police have told me about the allegation. The parent or other appropriate adult is allowed in to see the child at this point too.

In law, 'appropriate adult' means someone who is there 'to safeguard the interests of children and young persons detained or questioned by police officers', and is generally a parent or guardian, someone from social services, or a community volunteer. They will have been allowed to see the child for the process of booking in at the very beginning – under law this can only happen when the appropriate adult has arrived – but after that, the adult could be left sitting out in the waiting room for hours. Occasionally, if the station is quiet, the child is particularly young or vulnerable, and the crime is deemed minor, a parent might be allowed to sit with the child in a front room instead, but this is rare. So by this stage, depending on the adult's own emotional state, bringing them into the room can be beneficial or detrimental. They might calmly ask their child what happened, but I see everything from a reassuring hug, to a furious telling off, as emotions are understandably heightened.

After the initial catch-up, I will ask the adult to leave the room again, as now I need to get as much information as possible from my client about their understanding of the situation, as well as try to learn more about them, their character and their background. I am piecing together a picture that will help me decide the next steps to take for the interview.

The fact that I want to do this alone can confuse, and initially anger a lot of parents. 'This is my child, why can't I be here? I have every right to know what is going on!' is a common response. I can understand why they feel like that, but it is imperative they leave for two very good reasons.

The first one – and I have found that a lot of people don't know this – is that parents and appropriate adults are not protected by legal privilege, so they can be compelled to give evidence about what they hear in that room. Legal professional privilege is a rule in law that protects communications between a lawyer and client when they are being given legal advice. It means that unless the client actually wants any of their conversations to be shared with others, they remain private, and a court cannot ask for them to be revealed. The same rule, however, does not cover anyone else in the room at the time, so can you imagine being called up to the stand and asked what your child said, when you and they thought it was a protected, private conversation?

I am aware of a murder case in which a girl had killed her uncle, who had been sexually abusing her since she was twelve. The social worker was in the room when the girl was giving instruction, and was later compelled to give evidence about what she had heard, even though it went against everything she felt was right in her role. That was so incredibly difficult for her, and I never want anyone I am working with, or any parent, to end up in that situation.

The second reason is that, like it or not, children often don't tell me the truth in front of their parents. For a young person to trust me in that first meeting is not a given, but add the pressure of a parent also listening in to what can be a difficult conversation, and it becomes harder. Getting them to leave the room so it is only me they have to focus on, maximizes the chances of the young person telling me exactly what happened. There can be any number of reasons why they might lie or avoid telling me something in the presence of a parent, as their idea of what is important can be very different to mine. I'll give you an example.

I was called down to the station to assist Matt, a fourteen-year-old boy who had been brought in for interview by the police on an allegation of rape. His mum was also in the room as his appropriate adult when we began our initial conversation. It quickly became clear to me that the person making the allegation was the one who should have really been at the station, as everything actually pointed to the fact that a number of young boys had been brought to a house for the purposes of sexual exploitation. They had been given cannabis by adults and as the facts emerged they flagged a whole string of safeguarding issues.

But at this stage Matt was facing a really serious offence, and I had found out through disclosure that the police had established that he had been at the scene due to DNA on a cigarette butt. All Matt was focused on when we discussed this aspect though, was repeating: 'I don't smoke.'

It was obvious this was a lie and was only going to make him look guilty in interview. So eventually I asked for time alone with Matt, and was able to have a frank conversation with him, in which he admitted he had in actual fact been there and had been smoking, but as he had never told his mum he smoked, he hadn't wanted to admit to it in front of her. The fear of her finding out was overriding any awareness of the gravity of the wider situation he was in, which is typical of so many children. They respond to the real-life situation in front of them, and don't see the bigger picture until it is spelled out to them – in this case that people would take the implication of his fib to be that he was then lying about everything else. Eventually Matt admitted to smoking, his version of events was accepted and the charges were dropped, but not before he and all the children involved were charged and sent for trial.

This desire in children to cover up an aspect of their life they think won't go down well with their parents comes up quite regularly when a teenager has a boyfriend or girlfriend that their parents are unaware of, and who they were with at the time of the alleged crime. So when being questioned they won't raise their alibi as they don't want a parent to know, even though that would be the one thing that would close down the case instantly.

'I wasn't there, but I can't say where I was,' they say. Or even worse: 'I was there but didn't see what happened', even though they weren't there, but to them that seems easier than the truth. The idea of a crime that didn't involve them feels too abstract to be concerned about, whereas the potential wrath of their parent who is sitting right in front of them feels a lot more tangible.

I am not naive enough to think my own children would be any different – which is why I would definitely send a different lawyer along if they were to ever end up at the police station! I have two sons, and when my eldest turned ten, I put one of my business cards in the wallet he takes to school, and told him, 'If you or one of your friends get into trouble with the police, call me. It won't be me who deals with it, but one of my colleagues will come straight down and be there to help you.'

It is a given among all of us at JfKL that we would all represent each other's children if it was needed, and we don't need to know the conversations that are had behind closed doors. You need that person in there with your child to be someone who can take a step back, and a parent cannot.

So let's go back into the room with the child, where we are preparing for the police interview.

All lawyers who work with children develop their own method and style of speaking to them and in my case, the way I speak with the child will depend on their age and experience. I would say my approach is probably very different to traditionally trained lawyers, as my focus is on the child, building up a rapport with them and keeping things as simple, clear and straightforward as possible. I think about my own children and how I might explain something to them, and make a concerted effort to temper my language and use descriptions that make the experience more relatable to their everyday life. Unless they search out specific training, lawyers aren't taught how to speak with children, so often tend to overuse the legal jargon that is part of their everyday parlance, without allowing for their different audience. Time and again children who come to JfKL tell us they didn't understand what was being said to them by other legal professionals.

Ideally, I want to keep any long-term effect this experience might have on the child to a minimum. One of the ways I will do this is by suggesting that, rather than answering police questions, in interview we pull together a prepared statement addressing the accusation, and I read it on their behalf. We all know that the simplest or most unexpected thing can upset or antagonize a child, and that sort of response can be perceived negatively in court. They can get riled or confused by the police questioning, but on the other hand, children can also be quite compliant and suggestible. My aim is to avoid any of these reactions.

If I am short of information from the officer and the disclosure process has as good as disclosed nothing, I am in the dark, and will generally be planning to advise the client to give a 'no comment' interview, and I will read a statement on their behalf. There is a misperception that saying 'No comment' means you are guilty, whereas it can often be a way of protecting yourself. For example, imagine you were there when the crime was committed, but weren't involved. Even answering to confirm your whereabouts places you at the scene and strengthens the evidence the police have – they may not even have been sure of that fact at this stage. But it is tricky, as this is the client's first opportunity to outline a defence, and, ultimately, remaining silent in an interview can be used against the client in court. It is a fine line that both police officers and I are often trying to walk.

Once I have the facts and have worked out the next steps, I get the parent or appropriate adult back into the room to talk through what I am advising the child to do. Some lawyers fail to do this, but I don't think it is helpful to have the parent sitting in the interview worrying or getting angry at the route we are taking, simply because they have been left in the dark about the reasons behind the direction and decisions.

The Formal Police Interview

Then it is time to go in for the formal interview. This is held in a small, often too stuffy or too cold room, the officers sitting on one side of the table on chairs, my client and I left to sit on the other side on a backless bench, with the appropriate adult. Everything is fixed to the floor; the aim is clearly not to make you feel comfortable, and there is generally nothing homely about these interview rooms at all. The interview might be recorded on camera, but most of the time it is audio only, recorded onto CDs, with three copies made – one sealed for the court, one kept by the police, and one for me as the lawyer to take away.

The interview starts with a lot of introductions, in which my client is asked to confirm their name and address, then the officer explains who everyone in the room is, and talks about an individual's rights to legal advice.

When I introduce myself, I use it as a chance to lay out the direction I want the interview to take, for the benefit of both the officer and my client. So I might say something like: 'I'm Aika Stephenson from Just for Kids Law. For the benefit of my client and the tape I'd like to remind my client I will continue to represent you through this interview and will intervene if questioning is inappropriate or oppressive, although I am sure that won't happen today! You can ask to stop the interview at any point and everyone else has to leave the room and we can have a consultation.'

I will also flag up the route we are taking, such as a 'no comment' interview or that I will read a statement, so the officer knows what we are planning. This is also another opportunity to remind the young person, who might be feeling very overwhelmed, of what we are doing.

Then it is time for the official police caution, which may as well be in an alien language as far as most children are concerned:

'You do not have to say anything. But, it may harm your defence if you do not mention when questioned something which you later rely on in court. Anything you do say may be given in evidence.'

How do you make that comprehensible to a child? Let's look at it in sections.

So, the first phrase: 'You do not have to say anything' – basically you are not obliged to say anything to the police – although in practice most young people don't believe that. They think you do have to speak when a police officer speaks to you, and in the majority of life situations they would be right, as more often than not it will cause more problems to keep quiet or ignore the police. That in itself is a bit of a conundrum for a child to get their mind around, as you will see from some examples given later.

The middle phrase: 'But, it may harm your defence if you do not mention when questioned something which you later rely on in court' – is hugely problematic. Try explaining to an eleven year old, 'You have to tell me now whether you have a defence, because if you don't say something in the police station, if your case goes to court, they might be less likely to believe you are telling the truth as you didn't mention it before.' It is nonsensical to them. It's actually hard for most adults to comprehend. What does it even mean, a case going to court? Getting young children to understand the situation without terrifying or confusing them further is quite complicated.

And then the last sentence: 'Anything you do say may be given in evidence' – well, the police will remember what you tell them, so we need to be careful that you say the right thing.

As part of the preparation for the interview I will have run through this caution with the child and will have done my best to make sure they comprehend the implications. I ask them three questions to determine that they have understood it.

- **Do you have to speak to the police?** The answer needs to be 'No' if they have understood this

- **What happens to what you do say to the police?** I'm looking for an answer such as 'It will be recorded' or 'It becomes evidence'

- **If you don't speak today, but you then tell your story in court, what might they think?** Ideally the young person will answer, 'That I am lying, because I didn't say this before' or 'They might not believe me'

It is the measure of a good police officer if they also do something similar during the interview, and if they don't, I will often pull them up, saying, 'I think you need to explain that again, don't you?'

Once the caution has been dealt with, this is the point at which the interview finally officially starts, and anything after that point can be used as evidence in court. In the majority of cases I end up reading a statement on my client's behalf. At times the statement might be long and packed with detail, and an officer will hear it and say something like, 'That was very compelling, you have dealt with everything I had to ask, so we can conclude this interview.' Other times the statement might be as short as: 'I deny the offence. I have not been given enough disclosure, but I want to put on record that I am not accepting it.' Then, even though I have told them the client will be doing a 'no comment' interview, the officer starts asking questions.

This can be tricky if the child decides to start speaking and goes against my advice, but younger children especially struggle with the balance of power when an officer asks them questions. Not replying or saying 'No comment' is an alien concept. One technique I have developed with young people who struggle to stay quiet is to have a 'code' between us, that pulls their mind back to the guidance of not speaking. I can't openly nudge them, and while I can speak up and say, 'I'd like to remind my client of the legal advice that was given to them', I can only intervene two or three times before I would be considered to be disrupting the interview. So the code could be something as simple as me tapping my pen on the table three times.

A client whose case appeared on my desk in the early days of JfKL, and who struggled with the idea of remaining silent, was Toby, an eleven-year-old boy who I accompanied to an interview at Paddington Green Police Station in London.

Toby had been called in for interview after a playground fall in which a girl lost her front teeth. She was much taller than her peers and used to pat the boys, including Toby, on the head to joke about their height, so one day they decided to bundle her in revenge. As she fell, she knocked out her teeth. Of course, it wasn't the smartest decision by the boys, and her parents were understandably furious, but was it really a criminal matter, or should an apology and parental/school punishment have been enough?

Her parents thought the former, and reported the incident to the police, so I found myself in the station with Toby, dealing with the interview. Trying to explain to a child what the term 'assault' actually means, and how best to react to the questions around it in a police interview is incredibly difficult. In these situations, with a particularly young and confused child, we are relying on the police to handle the questioning appropriately – using language, tone and a level of detail that is fitting to the child's age and state of mind.

I had decided that reading a statement on Toby's behalf would be the simplest and most effective way forward, and hopefully cause the least stress for him. I pulled the statement together from our conversation, and felt confident it would explain everything he had told me about how the incident came about – that they were mucking around, and never intended to actually hurt the girl and essentially it was an accident. Then I told him not to say anything, and even if the officer started asking questions, he was to say 'No comment'.

But in the reality of the situation, despite rehearsing beforehand, Toby, as is the case for so many children, had a deep-rooted understanding that it was rude not to answer an adult, let alone a police officer, so he kept speaking. Despite my best efforts to rein it in, the questions kept coming, leaving him increasingly stressed, intimidated and confused.

Then the officer pulled out photos of the girl's injured mouth, and asked: 'Don't you feel bad about this, and what you have done?'

Toby was visibly upset by this stage, and I was furious at how it was being handled. I pulled the officer to one side and tried to reason with him: 'Did you never bundle anyone when messing around as a child? Can you not see this was ill-thought-out, childish fun with an unfortunate outcome?' But it was as if he couldn't relate to his younger self at all, and didn't want to engage.

A child ending up in court thanks to an accidental playground tumble, or a misthrown item in a game of catch, happens more than you might imagine. Parents can insist a child is arrested for what is effectively playground boisterousness. The police have to take complaints seriously, when the reality is that most parents don't really want to see another child with a criminal record, they just want to see them told off by someone in authority.

Poor Toby was already petrified at the idea of being called in by the police, but it was worse when he realized where we were. At that time, Paddington Green was well known in the news and to local residents, as the headquarters of anti-terrorism policing operations. People such as the suspects in the 7/7 London bombings, and Brits released from Guantanamo Bay had been kept there, and Toby kept asking me: 'Are there terrorists here?'

By formalizing the process, and effectively making a young person into a suspect, it made the incident seem far more serious than it should be. Then everyone feels as though they have to start going through the process, focusing on box-ticking for their job, and not really standing back and looking at the bigger picture. Thankfully, in the end someone at the Crown Prosecution Service (CPS), the government agency that decides which cases are prosecuted or not, saw sense and no further action was taken against Toby.

That horrendous style of questioning is unfortunately not a rare occurrence, and at times I can only wonder if the officer has left his empathy at the door. Other times, the questioning in the interview can become highly inappropriate, and officers seem to forget that they are dealing with a child.

For example, I was called in to support a boy with severe learning difficulties who had been brought in to the station on allegations that he had touched girls inappropriately. His mum had not yet spoken to him about sex, and his understanding of it was basic to none, but the officer was asking overtly sexual questions that were incredibly confusing to the boy – and offensive to his mum. It was effectively as if this boy was getting his sex education through a police interview. I paused the interview and had a very difficult conversation with the officer about how inappropriate his line of questioning had become, and eventually he backed off. But I do wonder if sometimes an officer's focus on the end result gets in the way of their sense of humanity.

Formally suspending an interview is not technically the role of a solicitor; it is my client who has the right to ask for this at any time, so that they can speak to me. But obviously with children it can sometimes get to the point where I feel I have no other choice. I can't terminate an interview, though, simply request a pause, before the interview starts up again.

Once the interview ends, I have a debrief with my client. At this point, a decision has to be made by the police about whether to charge or bail, and if it looks set to be a quick decision or if the young person might need help getting home, I will wait. However, the fees are so stiff for a police interview, and my workload is so high back at the office, that waiting for what could be hours isn't viable.

The child is returned to the cell while awaiting a decision. The police have twenty-four hours to keep them there, or it can be extended to seventy-two hours if certain criteria are met.

Unless the officer decides there is no case, the young person will be:

- charged and remanded in custody overnight to appear in court the next day

- or charged and bailed to attend court in a couple of weeks

- or bailed to return to the station while an investigation is ongoing

- or released under investigation

Incredibly, sometimes the decision on whether to charge or not can take a year, and I have to keep writing letters and chasing up. But obviously, ideally it will be much sooner.

But what happens when the child hasn't been formally arrested, but is simply asked to come into the station? 'Hi, Mrs Harrison, this is PC Jones. We would like to talk to your son about an incident that occurred in the park on Friday. Would you be able to bring him down to the station for a conversation?'

It's not a phone call that parents want to receive, but at the same time there's nothing that sounds threatening about it. Often a child will be invited down to the police station 'for a conversation' about an incident. A parent interprets that as a relaxed request, and of course their child has reassured them they are innocent, so they think, 'Well, a quick chat with that friendly sounding policeman will get this all cleared up.' In reality, it is a very misleading phrase, and no parent who hears it should ever treat it as 'just a conversation'. My advice, as you will see throughout this book, is to always seek legal representation, even at this stage, as before you know it the situation can rapidly spiral out of control.

Similarly, there is a misconception that if the police officer is conducting an interview at a person's home, it means it is definitely just a 'chat' and not a legal proceeding. We have had calls from parents when their child is in the middle of talking to an officer, and they have suddenly realized that this is a serious matter, and the child is speaking under caution. There is very little we can do at this stage – we can't undo it, as a formal system is now underway.

If a child is being interviewed under caution as a suspect, that means a legal process has started and it's expected that they are involved in a criminal offence – and their parents need to make a lawyer the first point of call. If they haven't committed an offence, sometimes people wonder why a lawyer is necessary, but it is just as crucial whether the person knows they are guilty or not. At this stage, everyone needs to understand the importance of outlining their defence and what their defence is. Obviously, defences have a legal element to them that children don't understand and, despite their best intentions, nor do parents most of the time. Depending on the circumstances, a young person may, for example, need to explain why they reacted in a way that could be perceived as aggressive or violent: 'I was in fear for my safety'; 'I used reasonable force'; 'I didn't carry on beyond restraining that person or doing whatever it was that was needed for my own well-being'. People love the phrases 'self-defence' and 'reasonable force', but do you really know what they mean in the eyes of the law? Probably not, which is where a lawyer comes in.

Lawyers are also key in looking for out-of-court disposals – that is to say, ways in which any minor crime that a young person commits can potentially be dealt with without going to court. There are a number of methods that I'll come to later. The important thing about out-of-court resolutions is that the process is much less stressful, and the child ends up without a criminal conviction.

Sometimes the police will genuinely not want to charge the child, as they realize for whatever reason it is not in the best interest of the child to have this particular crime on their criminal record. Perhaps they are aware they don't have enough evidence to charge them, and if the child doesn't say anything, the case isn't going anywhere. But parents, thinking their child is innocent and trusting the legal process, will tell them: 'Go in and tell the police officers everything, sit down and tell the truth', without understanding they might just have set the wheels in motion for a damaging legal case ahead.

A police officer can tell the lawyer off the record that they have no evidence, and that minimal response from the defendant would be the best route, but they can't say that to the suspect themselves. Unfortunately there have been quite a few situations in which we have come in after the initial interview and the child has already acknowledged events, without accepting the legal implications of doing so. At that stage, I have no choice but to start preparing them for court.

When he was fourteen years old, Chris was asked in for interview about an incident on a bus a few weeks before. He was adamant that he was innocent, and his parents did exactly as so many do – they thought it would be a simple conversation and everything would be cleared up. His apparent crime was throwing an empty plastic bottle at a girl on the school bus. She had been in a dispute with some other girls, a dispute that he wasn't involved in, when the claim was he threw the bottle which then hit her. She had not sustained any injuries, and while Chris accepted he had thrown a bottle, he said it was at a friend, and the bottle only made contact with his friend, not the girl. Even setting aside the fact of whether it made contact or not, the general consensus would be that it was silly behaviour, but hardly criminal. However it turned out to be a classic case of thinking it would be too ridiculous to go anywhere … then down at the police station and unrepresented, before you know it, he was charged with common assault by beating.

That is when his mum contacted us, and we wrote representations on his behalf to the prosecution to say it really wasn't in the public interest to push ahead with this case. The boy had never been in trouble before, lived at home with his parents and siblings, and had a clean school record. What could possibly be achieved by pushing ahead and taking this to trial? It didn't help the prosecution's case that they had only decided to pull the boy in for questioning more than twenty-eight days after the incident, when CCTV from the bus cameras, that could have settled the matter, had been deleted.

I was infuriated when I got the response, and was told the decision had been made by the CPS that the case needed to be heard in a magistrates' court. Thankfully, once there, the magistrates saw sense and Chris was acquitted, but it was farcical to spend thousands of pounds of public money on this prosecution. I'm not suggesting the situation should be ignored altogether – if the girl was upset by the incident, and her parents were concerned about her being bullied at school in general, then that absolutely needed to be addressed. But is it really something that should be dealt with through the court system?

I think there is a lack of understanding as to what it means when you press charges against a child. Keep in mind that ten is the age of criminal responsibility, i.e. the age at which children are considered to be capable of a crime, and can therefore be arrested and charged.

But irate parents might demand a school does something about an incident, the school doesn't want to get involved, so the parents call the police, and an officer, once called, has to go through a formal process. So, before you know it, what should probably have been dealt with via a school detention or the like, has become full-blown legal proceedings.

Then there is the potential harm it did to Chris's well-being. It worries me that for children like him who have grown up trusting police officers and the law, going through something like this diminishes that belief and faith in the system. They feel as though, 'Oh, the police are accusing me of something I haven't actually done. Maybe they aren't here to help me after all,' and that relationship is tainted for ever.

Some of my clients have said, 'I used to want to be a police officer, but I don't anymore', which is very sad. Even worse, many of my clients tell me they wouldn't call the police now even if they were in trouble, which is frightening. If that is genuinely how our young people feel, we really do have a problem.

This case was relatively quick – six months between the incident and the trial – but that's still six months that this fourteen-year-old had the case hanging over his head. Is that fair?

Sadly, this is not a one-off. I am regularly contacted about similar incidences that should never reach the levels they do. When we know that courts are being stretched to breaking point, what is being achieved and who is making these decisions?

Children in Cells

This idea of police asking children in for a conversation at the station was partly due to an increased understanding that children don't necessarily need to be arrested and taken to a custody suite in order to get answers. Coming in voluntarily at a time that suits all parties can be much better for the child in the long term. Just one night in a police cell can be highly damaging to a child, and can even be the trigger that pushes them towards crime. The law itself recognizes that police cells are traumatic, inappropriate places for children and that police forces and local authorities have a duty to transfer children to more appropriate settings. Unfortunately the official guidance is not always followed, and too often children end up spending the night in police cells after they have been arrested.

This is why, in 2016, JfKL started a campaign called No Child In Cells, which has been ongoing ever since. We have been campaigning for change, bringing a series of legal challenges against police forces and local authorities concerning the unlawful detention of children in police cells overnight. As a result, various local councils have had to review their policies on the treatment of children in police custody. There was a lot of press coverage about the issue, and in October 2017 the UK government introduced national guidance for police forces and local authorities in England on their responsibilities towards children in custody. The Home Office Concordat on Children in Custody makes clear that police cells are inappropriate places for children and should only be used to hold children for short periods of time when no alternative is available.

It states:

> A night in a cell is an intimidating experience.
> Police custody facilities are designed to detain
> adults suspected of criminal activity, and they
> offer little in the way of comfort or emotional
> reassurance. For a child – especially one
> deprived of familial support – a prolonged stay
> in this environment can be harmful.

Since this guidance was published, there has been a reduction in the number of children being held overnight in police cells, although in 2019 the figure for children being held in London was over 7,000 – still unacceptably high, and the reason why we can't yet let up on the issue.

It becomes more complicated as holding children overnight in a cell is not always a decision made by the police – sometimes local authorities have left them with no choice. The police have a duty to transfer children to local authority accommodation once they are charged with an offence, to avoid them spending more time in police cells. But local authorities often fail to provide the required accommodation. Of those 7000-plus children held overnight in 2019, more than 1,000 of them had been charged, so should have been in local authority accommodation.There is no secure accommodation for children in London at all. Somewhat incredibly, the nearest secure children's home is in Lincolnshire. This makes it nearly impossible for the police to move a child to a secure home in time, leaving hundreds of children to spend the night locked up.

JfKL took one local authority to court over the issue after a child was kept in custody for two nights, despite police requests that she be moved. But while the local authority accepted in court that the system was unsatisfactory, the court dismissed the claim, saying that it '… is really a complaint about the nationwide lack of secure accommodation available to all local authorities due to the absence of funding by Central Government.'

Perhaps it is, but does that mean we should keep quiet, and that it's okay for things to continue as they are?

It is clear there have been lessons learned and the police, on the whole, have come round to the way of thinking that there are plenty of times when it really isn't necessary to have children in custody. But it is still an area I feel very strongly needs a lot more improvement and change. The fact we still have children who are arrested and kept in custody for twenty-four hours before any action is taken is not acceptable. Just for Kids Law is continuing to push police forces and local authorities to sign up to the Concordat and follow the law as well as official guidance. We will carry on with our campaign until no child suffers the trauma of a night in a police cell.

The Police as a Whole

Being completely honest, I don't think highly of the police at all, which is a sad situation. My work is based mainly in London, so I am dealing with the Metropolitan Police (commonly known as the Met), and it may well be that my views are skewed because of that. I'm told by some officers from outside London that they don't agree with the Met's approach, and that they do things differently. That may well be the case, but I can only talk about what I know. It feels like there are a lot of issues when it comes to power … and, of course, racism – although I will revisit that in a later chapter.

While I don't want to be completely scathing about the police – some of it is a personality thing – the force often attracts a certain sort of person, whether we like to admit that or not. I think there are issues with what draws people to the police force, their backgrounds and qualifications. There seems to be a lack of empathy, and sadly there aren't many members of the police who I feel have gone into the force for the right reasons. Some of it is just the system that they are having to work within, which I honestly don't feel is fit for purpose, combined with a lack of training. Many of the officers I have come across seem to have very little understanding of how to work with young people, and of their duties when it comes to interviewing and investigating them. Occasionally you get one who is higher ranking, often older, and who wants to assist, resolve the issue and get the best outcome, but it really feels rare.

There is a general attitude from officers that they are above other people and shouldn't need to temper their behaviour as they are 'the authority'. While there is a move to try to change that conduct now, it is getting to a dangerous point, with reports repeatedly pointing to the fact that the general public are losing trust in the police. Surveys conducted by the polling organization YouGov indicate a loss of public confidence in the police:

- YouGov's monthly tracker 'Are the police doing a good job?' shows that over the course of 2020 an average of 70 per cent of respondents thought the police were doing a good job relative to 21 per cent who thought they were doing a bad job. However, by April 2023 these figures were 47 per cent and 44 per cent respectively.

- Similarly, the proportion of people who had not very much confidence or no confidence at all in the police to deal with crime averaged 38 per cent in 2020. As of April 2023, this figure had risen to 53 per cent.

I had one case where an officer was arresting a client, who claimed that the officer had been unnecessarily provoking him. Whatever the background to the situation, though, as the officer went to arrest him, my fifteen-year-old client spat at him. In his report, the officer wrote:

> I felt disgusted. My instinctive reaction was to throw out my hand and punch him directly in the face.
>
> He said 'I'm bleeding you punched me' and was quite shocked.
>
> I replied with words I believed would be impactful and the defendant would understand, which were something to the effect of: 'Yes because you spat on me you disgusting little c*nt.'

I would never defend spitting at someone, and think it's a horrible thing to do, so maybe some people would think my client got what he deserved with that punch. But to me this isn't a brawl on the street; the police aren't allowed to punch people, let alone children, and an officer should have been capable of handling the incident in a professional manner and rising above it. It is part of their training.

The fact that he wrote that statement, which was to end up in court, and that the CPS didn't think it was an issue, gave me real insight into the police's understanding of what is acceptable these days. The officer didn't get into any trouble, yet my client was in court for obstructing the police and assaulting an officer. Are they no longer meant to be controlled, law-abiding citizens themselves? Thankfully, the magistrates saw the incident for what it was, and acquitted my client at trial.

I have had plenty of situations where members of the police have been everything from deliberately obstructive to just plain petty towards me, too. I remember once going to a police station and it was immediately clear that they didn't like my client and the fact that I was actually attempting to defend him seemed to annoy them. I was taking some information from the custody record and left my pencil case on the front desk, and realized as soon as I left. But when I went back to retrieve it they claimed I hadn't left it, then I saw it behind them in the bin. Petty power plays like that really get on my nerves – and again, what does it say about the mentality of the people who are meant to be exemplary members of society?

I honestly think the entire policing system needs a complete overhaul, but this kind of culture is deeply embedded and it could take decades to change. There is a whole movement around defunding the police which I am interested in. It began in the USA, and is focused around the idea that money should be moved away from the police forces, and instead put into initiatives that are tackling crime at its roots and through the community. But it is still in its infancy, so let's see how it unfolds. For now, I need to focus on helping the children who are in the current system for as long as it exists.

CHAPTER 2

Up in Court

'So, tell me a bit about your parents,' I asked Jordan, a thirteen-year-old boy I was to represent in the magistrates' court that morning. He shifted in his seat, and mumbled a reply, too quiet to hear. As I encouraged him to repeat his reply, two girls sat down on the hard plastic chairs next to me, and in silence started messaging on their phones. Not quite the privacy we needed for a difficult conversation, and my chance to get the information I needed from Jordan instantly became slimmer. I signalled to him to follow me over to another set of seats, hidden in the far corner, avoiding the two boys who were starting to trade insults near the door. Jordan and I had only met that morning, and I had just a short time to work out what I was to say in court to help minimize the sentence he was to receive for fighting with another boy. He had decided to plead guilty, but it was down to me to offer mitigation, so the more I could understand about his life away from this one incident, the better.

The paperwork from the prosecution had only arrived in my inbox the evening before and I had studied it to see what the police officer's take on the incident was. But right now I wanted to know more about the impact on Jordan of something his Youth Offending Team officer had mentioned earlier: Jordan had been in care for a while last year, before returning to his mum's home, and I needed to hear from him how it had impacted on his life.

'Well, I guess when my mum …'

'Are you ready to go in next?' a court-list caller interjected, keen to keep that day's clients flowing through the court.

I sighed and, shaking my head, told her no, that in fact I needed time to actually speak to my client in private.

As she headed off, a disappointed look on her face, I was sure she was about to move us right to the bottom of the list so we would have the opposite problem and be hanging around all day instead.

I'd love to say this was an exceptional circumstance, that the normal court process is a slick machine that offers everyone involved the necessary time and support to get to the truth. But it wouldn't be true – I'd be sugarcoating a system that in reality feels like it is at breaking point.

I hate to break it to you, but if you are a fan of the likes of *Ally McBeal, Suits, The Good Fight, Law and Order* … appearing in court is nothing like you might imagine. In fact, all these American legal dramas have a lot to answer for, in giving the British public quite a skewed idea of how the criminal justice system in the UK works. I watch far too many of them myself, too – my partner can never understand how I spend all day dealing with the law, only to then come home and watch fictional characters from within that world – but the reality is very different.

I want to talk you through how the court system really works (and how it doesn't), from the lead-up to a first appearance, and in the courtroom itself, from the people involved, to some of the myths and problems we encounter every day.

Youth Court

Particularly serious crimes tend to end up at a Crown Court (see Chapter 11), but for the majority of cases where a child under eighteen is the defendant, they will be heard at a youth court.

Youth courts can deal with a large spectrum of offences from serious violent and sexual offences to shoplifting. They are housed in the same buildings as the magistrates' court for adults, with the main differences between the two being:

- The public aren't allowed to attend, although a child of sixteen and under must have an adult with them

- The defendant's name and photo cannot be revealed outside the court, except in exceptional circumstances

- The atmosphere *should* be less formal in areas such as language and dress and the layout of the court room, to avoid the child feeling intimidated, and encourage them to participate

- The focus should be on rehabilitation rather than retribution

- The youth court can sentence a child to up to two years in custody whereas the maximum for an adult in the magistrates' court is twelve months

But Before You Even Get Into the Courtroom ...

When a lawyer agrees to represent someone in court, people imagine we have had weeks to prepare, time to work through the papers from the prosecution, developing a well-researched defence, full of case law and evidence compiled from time spent with the defendant and witnesses.

The reality is very different. Papers from the prosecution are often not received until the day before, or even the morning of the court appearance, and there is a reasonable chance we have never met the defendant until then, particularly if they were only arrested the day before.

In fact, much of the pre-trial preparation is done in the court waiting room or café. This is because, while court facilities can vary wildly, many of the buildings are very old and, shockingly, there are plenty without interview rooms where a defence lawyer can speak with their client in private and take their instructions.

There was one inner city court, which has thankfully now closed, which used to have a waiting area with a TV, and everyone would be huddled in corners trying to chat with their young clients while Jeremy Kyle was blaring out of the screen above. It was a very depressing place.

A speech and language therapist who was giving evidence for us recently was so horrified by the lack of rooms and facilities in the court she attended, she was sending photos to her colleagues in disbelief at the set-up.

Another court I regularly attend only has an interview room available for the duty solicitor (i.e. the solicitor employed by the court to deal with clients who attend without a lawyer), and other than that you are expected to use the now-closed café, where they have left the tables and chairs behind. There is hardly any more privacy there than in the waiting area, and there will be lawyers with their clients on the adjacent tables, so the idea of client confidentiality goes out of the window.

There might even be solicitors for your client's co-accused around – and if you have a conflict of interest between clients, you definitely don't want them to know what you are discussing with your client.

Equally, it can be a sensitive conversation, in which you are trying to help that young person make a decision on whether to plead guilty or not. The system is geared up to give people credit for what is known as not wasting court time – that is to say, pleading guilty at your first appearance, as opposed to down the line, or waiting to be found guilty. You could get a 25 to 30 per cent reduction on your sentence at this stage. But that is a lot for a young person to take in, understand, and decide on in some noisy court waiting area, so it can be difficult.

Then, if a young person has decided to plead guilty, you need to discuss mitigation with them, which is where I get the chance to tell their story, with the aim of reducing a potential sentence. I am asking them to disclose very personal things about their family circumstances, education, trauma they might have experienced – just the kind of conversations I was trying to have with Jordan at the start of this chapter. So many of these waiting areas are far from ideal settings to get someone to open up to you on such private matters, when anyone might be listening in, and the constant distractions mean that I might miss something.

Most youth courts open at 9.30 a.m., with the magistrates sitting from 10 a.m. to 5 p.m. with an hour's lunch break in the middle of the day. Before the Covid pandemic changed the system, everyone would be bailed to arrive at 9.30 a.m., but you could end up first in the courtroom or last. Obviously, from my end I want to work out a plan with my client as soon as possible, so we are prepared for whenever we are called. There is a list caller, whose job it is to get everyone through court in as timely a manner as possible, so inevitably they are constantly putting pressure on you – 'Are you ready yet?' – while I have to push back until I really feel we are. Thankfully, since Covid though, in many courts they have been doing staggered listings, so there are fewer people in the court waiting areas at the same time. Most of the legal profession are hopeful this is a system that will remain.

It is a strange mix when it comes to the atmosphere in the waiting area. Some days it can be calm and smooth sailing, with everyone just wanting to get their cases over and done with. But other times, understandably, emotions are high and tensions can boil over. Parents who have come along can get irritated, especially if they are waiting for hours and have work or other commitments to get off to. Then the young person can become frustrated or upset, walk out of court and I need to go and find them and talk them around. I can find myself juggling the task of managing an angry parent, impatient court staff and a young person's expectations and feelings, before I've even entered the courtroom.

Perhaps unsurprisingly then, at times it can feel a bit like the Wild West with an undercurrent of tension that can boil over and turn into violence. I've had clients beaten up in the waiting area, one who was ambushed while we were in consultation. In another case, people were waiting outside to attack my client after his hearing, so we had to get him out of a back entrance and into a taxi. There is security on hand to help, but the level of competence can vary quite wildly.

Part of the reason for these outbreaks of violence is that courts now deal with more people from multiple boroughs on the same day. In the past they dealt with cases from the same location on a given day, so cases from Enfield might be heard one day, and those from Westminster on another. This made sense in terms of staffing and the people needed at court, but pressures put on the system by the closure of magistrates' courts and a reduction in court time means more young people are being pushed together in fewer venues. This means there is a higher chance of people from areas that sometimes historically have tensions with other areas being cooped up together. They are hanging around, frustrated and nervous, and their feelings spill over.

The organization of court appearances leaves a lot to be desired. During the pandemic things went particularly haywire. No one was answering emails or phone calls, people would be sent to the wrong courts, no barrister would be available to cover a case even when it had already been given to the chambers … They were so overstretched and understaffed. But at least there was an excuse for this chaos during the pandemic. However, the court system is embarrassingly inefficient at the best of times, in my opinion, and the aftermath of Covid, with the huge backlog of cases, means it now seems officially broken.

In the Courtroom

The layout of a youth court is in theory meant to give off a more informal vibe than a magistrates' court, and certainly to make it look a lot more relaxed than a Crown Court.

The magistrates sit up the front at the bench, with the prosecuting and defence lawyers facing them, and the defendant and their parent or legal guardian are supposed to sit next to them. Children under sixteen must have an adult who sits with them throughout the proceedings, but if they are sixteen or seventeen they can choose whether they want to have this or not.

There are clear practice directions that say a child should be able to sit next to their lawyer, as opposed to standing in the dock, but whether this is followed varies across the country. I can be in court one day and, without me saying anything, the legal advisor will tell the young person, 'Sit next to your lawyer, and you don't need to worry about standing until we are finished'. Then the next day I'll be elsewhere and they are told, 'Into the dock, and stand when you are addressing the court.' It feels like those second types of court are still stuck on the idea that this is a punishment, whereas it is never supposed to have been about that with children. The focus should *always* be on rehabilitation and prevention of offending.

Other than that, the only other people in the room might be someone from the Youth Offending Team, the court clerk/legal advisor who looks after all the paperwork and clarifies the law for the magistrates, an usher, and at the point of giving evidence, any witnesses or victims.

The Magistrates

At a youth court there is no jury. Instead, the case is heard by three magistrates who decide on the young person's guilt or innocence, and determine the sentence or next steps.

The magistrates are not legally trained or paid, but have gone through several days of specific training for this role, and are considered to be upstanding members of the community. The one sitting in the middle is the more senior of the three.

The role of the magistrate is to listen to the evidence, interact with the young person, and help make a decision on the next course of action. At times it might be a district judge (DJ) in charge, who, unlike a magistrate, is paid and legally trained. Some courts keep their DJs for the more serious cases, while in others they will work their way through the full remand list, so there is no way to be sure ahead of a court hearing who you will end up with.

The magistrates will not be wearing robes or gowns, nor – contrary to popular belief – will they be using a gavel. That is not something that has ever been used in youth courts (or any court in Britain for that matter), and once again is an erroneous stereotype that owes itself to popular culture. They will address the young person directly by their first name, again to keep it more informal, and ask them if they plead guilty or not guilty.

The type of magistrates who, in my opinion, do the best jobs, are those who try to engage with the child on the child's own level, who aim to be trauma-informed, and realize that it may be difficult for a young person to speak up in this alien situation. They want to make it as painless as possible for them, in the hope that they will open up and engage with the process.

I think people forget that the traditional expectations put on a child in court might not be fair. They can be judged by a number of superficial factors, whereas, in the life of some of our clients, the court is actually the least of their worries. For example, I might have a client going through a really traumatic period, who walks into court with their hood up, and just wants to recoil from the world – they aren't trying to be rude, they are just trying to get by, and their attire might be a security blanket for them. If the magistrate is instantly: 'Take your hood down, show some respect', and adopts a lecturing tone from the off, it can be very alienating. Surely it's better to engage with that young person?

If the magistrate goes straight in with something like, 'Stand up straight and look at me when you are speaking, don't you know where you are?' I know instantly it isn't going to go well.

Another question that always makes me wince is when they ask: 'Are you sorry?' That can be problematic as it is often a lot more complicated for the young person than that, but they tend to be more honest than an adult, who would probably claim that of course they were sorry, knowing this might lead to an easier ride. A child might get stuck and not know how to explain their feelings on the matter, leading to another lecture from the magistrate.

Some magistrates seem as though they have missed their calling, or love the sound of their own voice, and talk 'at' the child through a skewed, middle-class lens. I can only watch, uncomfortable, and just think, 'You haven't a clue.'

We had one particularly awful experience with a magistrates' court when one of our clients passed away while waiting for a court appearance on a minor charge. The circumstances of his death meant that a murder case had been opened. We wrote to the court to apprise them of the situation, but the charges against him couldn't just be dropped without a hearing to confirm that the case would be discontinued. At a time when the courts were particularly backlogged thanks to the pandemic, which had seen cases repeatedly cancelled with accused, witnesses and court staff down with Covid, and regulations slowing everything down, this seemed like a particularly ridiculous waste of time. But nevertheless a JfKL lawyer went along to the hearing.

Despite our previous contact, the information that our client had died clearly hadn't been passed on through the court, as the list caller kept coming out and calling his name. The lawyer tried to tell her that he wouldn't be there, but the caller persisted. Once in the court, the lack of sensitivity continued both from the prosecution and the bench. The lawyer was asked where her client was and explained he was deceased, as per our previous communication, and flagged that this was the whole reason this hearing had been requested.

The prosecutor asked for the death certificate, which we didn't have, and said they would need to check and confirm that our client had in fact died. The CPS were actually investigating his murder, and yet no one at their end seemed able to connect the dots between that case and this.

Then, to make matters worse, the magistrate began making jokes: 'We'd better inform the tagging company, as we don't want them turning up at his house to say he is in breach!'

It felt like a slap in the face, as though the system had no compassion for this young person, or for us as individuals. Lawyers will have varying degrees of relationships with their clients, and in our case it was a close one with this person. Appearing there that day and going through that hearing was difficult for our lawyer on a personal level, but that wasn't acknowledged or respected by the court at all. She was treated as just a part of the processing machine.

Alternatively, though, you can have great experiences where the magistrate shows exactly why they are in that role. One magistrate in a recent case started speaking to my client by asking what they liked to do when they weren't in court, and how their friends would describe them. They were genuinely interested in finding out about the young person, and getting a sense of them as more than just a one-dimensional 'naughty child'. It was a lot more impactful.

Sometimes a district judge might reserve a case to themselves, so that they create a dialogue with the young person, and say something like, 'I'm going to do a deal with you, I'm going to give you a chance to comply with the order, but I want you to come back and tell me how you're getting on,' and they will ask the child to come back every month for regular reviews. It's as though they have created a relationship, where the young person feels like they are in a contract with the judge – and every time I've seen that happen, it has gone well.

If the child has pleaded guilty, or been found guilty, there comes the point in the case when they are sentenced. The defence lawyer has given mitigation, and presented the magistrates or district judge with more information about the young person's background in an effort to reduce the sentence. This could be anything from good reasons why this offence will not be repeated, to remorse, or problems impacting on the child's personal life.

I've found that though there is quite an even male/female split among magistrates, they traditionally tend to be middle-aged or older, and from a white, middle-class background. Lately there has been a drive to open the role of magistrate out and make it more diverse. I believe they are succeeding in terms of race, sexuality, age, etc., but maybe less so in terms of background. It is such a crucial role in the life of a child, and, given that you don't need to be legally qualified, I'd encourage anyone who feels like they could make a real difference to look into volunteering for the role.

The Defence Lawyer

My job as a defence lawyer is to make sure my client's voice is heard, that their version of events is understood, and that if they are pleading guilty or found guilty, there is as much background information as possible given to the court. This is not to excuse, but to explain why they might have behaved in such a manner, and why the chances of reoffending are low.

In terms of how I carry out the role, I think I'm generally quite mild mannered – I'm definitely not one of those bolshy lawyers who come out aggressively fighting from the off. Instead, my main focus is to ensure the magistrate sees my client as simply a child and not a young offender. Often, young people in the youth justice system are seen as 'problem children', not just simply 'children'; or sometimes they aren't even viewed as children or young people, but as young adults. I've watched magistrates talk to a thirteen-year-old in a way that they would never speak to their own daughter of a similar age, as they perceive a child who is in court as streetwise and so therefore somehow older. It's for reasons such as this that I am so focused on trying to speak to the magistrates in a way that encourages them to connect with my client as a child.

In my mitigation I always try to tap into the personal and emotional side, and aim to arm myself with a great deal of information beforehand that shows the full picture of where my client is at in life. I try to pull the hearing back to looking at the case with a sense of humanity and the personal, rather than just the legal tick boxes. I am probably a bit braver in pushing that side than some other lawyers. Some people might describe it as 'bleeding heart', and I am definitely more flowery and emotional than those who just reel off the facts, but I don't think there's any harm in that, and I'd rather be accused of leaning more to a softer, liberal side, than the opposite.

Having said that, I am no walkover, and can be forceful when I disagree. There comes a point where the mild-mannered demeanour goes out of the window and the prosecution and magistrates realize that when it comes to defending my client's best interests, I will go all out. So much so, in fact, that I can risk getting myself into trouble ...

I was representing a fourteen-year-old boy who was in court on a charge of causing grievous bodily harm (GBH) by stabbing another boy with a compass. It had taken a long time to come to court, and in the interim my client had really engaged with the intervention programme of the Youth Offending Team; he had worked hard and was focused on turning his life around. He was a bright boy and had come far, and it felt as if the custodial sentence the magistrates were fixated on was going to undo all of that hard work. So, after I had said my part in mitigation, and the magistrates were discussing the sentencing, it felt like I hadn't been heard, that the compelling reasons I had presented were being ignored, so I stood up three more times to try different ways to get through to them. But it just wasn't working, and eventually the lead magistrate snapped: 'You are at risk of being in contempt of court – sit down and be quiet, or you will be joining your client in the cells!'

It was incredibly frustrating, but I'd tried everything I could – and of course they did send him to a young offender institution. His life has continued down that route so that, unfortunately, I've since represented him again. In my opinion, the magistrates missed their chance to rehabilitate and get this young person back on the right track, instead chosing to punish.

You might imagine that the first time I represented a client in court as their solicitor should be firmly imprinted on my brain, but, I'm ashamed to say, I don't remember it. Maybe because I had already been regularly appearing in court as a Youth Offending Team officer before my JfKL days, it wasn't such a standout moment for me. As a YOT officer, I had to present in court if I thought a young person should get bail. The solicitor would make the application, then I would say what I could offer, how I would supervise the child and why I thought they would comply. If they were being sentenced, I'd write the pre-sentence report.

When I became a solicitor, I would eagerly write up my submissions in advance. I'd read the prosecution papers, talk to the client, write out word for word what I wanted to say. Then, when it was time for me to address the court, deep breath, stand up, and work through it, with the papers in front of me as a prop, so I could go through them if I needed to organize my thoughts.

But now I read the papers, speak to a client beforehand, and formulate what I'm going to say, while rarely writing anything down. Clients can find it unnerving, and wonder how I'm going to know what to say, but I prefer to speak a bit more naturally from the heart, and besides, they don't realize how long I've been doing the job!

It is rare for me to get nervous in court these days, particularly magistrates' courts, although there will still be cases that bother me – in which I worry about presenting in the right way, or whether I've got the line quite right. And there always has been (and I imagine always will be) an adrenalin 'buzz' that pushes you on through the tougher cases.

What I *won't* be doing a lot of in court, is jumping up to say, 'Objection, your honour!' after every other question … This is another aspect of life in a courtroom that people have taken from TV shows, and they then assume you aren't doing your job properly if you don't do this. Put this one out of your mind – it doesn't happen!

The Role of the Prosecution Lawyer

The prosecution lawyer will take on the case and represent the state and victims of crime in the name of the King. They are legally qualified and working for the Crown Prosecution Service. They give the background on the crime from the police's viewpoint, and are effectively arguing that my client be prosecuted.

To me, my client is the most important person in that room, and as young people tend to see things in black and white, in their view the prosecutor is against them. When a prosecutor is running through the case, the version of events will be as the police officer perceived them, before there has been any legal challenge of those facts, so there might be information in there that the young person will disagree with. If I am too friendly or joking with the prosecutor, in the young person's eyes, it can be confusing. It can seem to them as though I am part of the system, when instead they want to feel that they have someone firmly on their side.

The same applies to the police – a young person can often become suspicious if they see you joking and chatting with the officer on their case, so I try not to overly engage, but to keep a professional, courteous relationship.

I always aim to have an open approach with the prosecutor, as it tends to make a working relationship run more smoothly. So, for example, if we are going for a guilty plea, I might have a frank discussion with the prosecutor about where they might be prepared to review a particular aspect or where there is room for manoeuvre. A straightforward prosecutor – who sees things for what they are – works best for me.

One time I had to say to a prosecutor in court, 'It is suggested that the police officer took cannabis from my client, but he doesn't seem to have exhibited it at all.'

She just looked at me, realized what a mistake had been made, and said, 'You would be right there, I'm offering no evidence.'

A prosecutor's day is very different from mine. I will be in court with just one or two clients to focus on, whereas they have to deal with everything in the court that day. Much of the time they will just be reading out case summaries from a long list, and they are under quite a lot of time pressure. As with all jobs, there are the good and the bad prosecutors. Some I find are just head down, going through the motions, and can come across as quite discourteous. Occasionally, if they haven't even made eye contact or acknowledged me in the court, I'll pull them up, saying: 'I'm doing my job, you're doing yours, there is no need to be so rude.' It can shock people, but again, I want to remind them that we are all human beings in that court, and though they are fulfilling their roles, some common decency – and an awareness of how important this case might be to a child's future – doesn't seem too much to expect.

Then there are others who are focused on getting through their nine-to-five list as fast as possible, and are not interested in the fight. They tend to agree to anything I suggest, just to get the case over quickly. So a conversation might go:

'My client will plead to this but not this, is that ok?'

'Yes, fine.'

'I'm going to apply for bail, can we agree to some conditions?'

'Yep, fine.'

In a way they are doing the right thing, as the role of a CPS lawyer is to remain more at arm's length from the case than a defence lawyer. They are presenting the prosecution case, but beyond that, don't see it as their battle. Obviously, this is beneficial to my client, so I'm always happy to come up against a prosecutor of this type.

Sometimes in court a prosecutor will have been unnecessarily awful, and when we come out, the young person says to me, 'That prosecutor hated me', which always upset me. No matter what your job is, no child should leave that room feeling that an adult in there had hated them.

We should be there for these young people, whichever side of the court system they are on, as they are still at that stage where their lives can be turned around, and they can be helped onto a more positive path. This really isn't the time to make them feel even worse about their situation.

There is one prosecutor who I regularly come across, who is good at her job and I like on a personal level, but who is a bit jaded by the system. When she sees one of the JfKL lawyers she will say: 'Oh, it's you guys, the ones who believe in unicorns. Your optimism and faith for the youth of today, knows no bounds ...'

She might see that as an insult, but to me it is a compliment – what's wrong with being optimistic about what young people can achieve?

What Exactly is the Crown Prosecution Service?

The Crown Prosecution Service (CPS) was created in 1986 with the aim of generating a greater consistency across the country in decision-making about whether a person should be prosecuted. The idea was also that, as an independent body separate from the police and government, the CPS could be more distant from a particular incident and make a more balanced decision as to whether there is a case to be answered or not.

The idea is that the CPS:

- decides which cases should be prosecuted
- determines the appropriate charges in more serious or complex cases and advises the police during the early stages of investigations
- prepares cases and presents them in court
- provides information, assistance and support to victims and prosecution witnesses

This means the CPS is involved with a case right from the point when a police officer believes a crime has potentially been committed. In some cases – the more minor ones, such as driving offences or common assault – the Evidential Review Officer at the police station may decide to drop the charges. This officer is a kind of 'gatekeeper'. But, more often than not, the case is referred to the CPS to determine the next step. The decision as to whether there is a case to be answered or whether there is nothing to it and it can be dropped, is made based on initial police investigations and the answers that have come out of police station interviews.

Assuming the case is referred on to the court, this is when I first hope to hear from the CPS, as they should be sending over the prosecution papers, so I have some basic understanding of the case and how it will be proceeding. Now, I'm just going to come out and say what I think here: the CPS isn't fit for purpose. Like every other public service, they are overstretched and as a result justice isn't served for anyone, whether that's victims or defendants.

The incompetency through much of the process is astounding. There are plenty of times when we have arrived at court and there were no case papers at all, meaning the case couldn't be heard, everyone had to come back the next week and try again, at which point there might be no papers again, as someone just didn't get around to compiling them. It is an annoyance for me but, much worse, it is distressing for a child and those around them, to build themself up for something that then gets delayed. At this point it takes a strong district judge to say this isn't good enough, and warn that if it happens once more, they will throw the case out altogether – something I have seen happen on several occasions.

This failure to do a job properly runs throughout the whole CPS. Take one of my cases where my client, Kyle, was arrested for possession of a knife. He had run into a shop, dashed behind the counter and dropped a knife on the floor. There is CCTV footage from inside the shop and you can see that he is absolutely petrified and has a bloodied nose.

From the outset he said that he had been attacked outside by a group of boys, one of them had pulled a knife but dropped it in the scuffle, and when Kyle had run for shelter into the shop he picked it up, explaining, 'If I took it with me, I knew no one could stab me with it.'

There was council CCTV from the road that covered the outside of the shop, and when Kyle was told the officers had seized that, he was relieved as he was sure it would vindicate him. But eighteen months later, and after four court appearances in which we were meant to be discussing evidence ahead of a trial being listed, the police had still not shared the CCTV with us. Of course we had said from the outset that we needed it, but it turned out the CPS couldn't get the footage into a downloadable format they could share with us. The judge was incredibly frustrated, as it was clearly pertinent to the case, and the case was at the point of going to trial without evidence.

Unfortunately we have a very traditional approach to prosecution in the British justice system, where the prosecutor holds all the evidence and as a defence lawyer you end up being reactive rather than proactive, as you are reliant on the prosecution for so much.

In practice, this means the police investigate the case and pass all of their investigation along to the CPS (at least, that's the theory, although there often seems to be a breakdown in this line of communication for whatever reason). Then the CPS decide what they disclose to the defence. There are meant to be two stages of disclosure: firstly, what they are going to rely on to prove the case; and secondly, whatever else they have in their possession that might assist or undermine the defence. If I choose to tell them the defence I am intending to use, they have another duty to review, which in fact is ongoing. It is quite antiquated and to some degree leaves the defence at the mercy of the CPS.

In the USA, they also have an investigator on the defence's side, so they will conduct their own investigation to find evidence to support the defendant's case, and there have been times when – in desperation – we have adopted this measure at JfKL. There is much I hate about the American legal system, but the proactive nature of defending your client without having to wait for or rely on the police, strikes me as a good thing. Constantly, I have to ask questions such as whether the police interviewed any other witnesses at the scene, or if there is CCTV, when it should simply be disclosed from the outset. I've reached the point of desperation at times and had to resort to going out knocking on doors, asking people if they have seen anything, or calling into pubs, asking to see their CCTV footage. But people aren't used to defence lawyers doing that, or asking them as a member of the public to make a statement, so they can be suspicious and close down. Helping the defence is not a culture that's encouraged in this country, and it would need a real shift in openness to the use of investigators for that to become easier.

I once had a young client involved in an incident on the King's Road in London, and he pointed out that the area was covered in CCTV, so there should be evidence to help support him on that front. But there was no disclosure of any CCTV, no references to police attempting to collect it, and my enquiries about it with the CPS elicited no results. In the end I went around the area taking photos of all the cameras, and sent them, along with a witness statement, to the CPS, asking how on earth it was possible they didn't have any footage whatsoever.

Places like pubs only keep their CCTV for a short time, generally between twenty-four hours and twenty-eight days, as it is for incidents such as pub fights or burglaries. So unless the police act quickly to get it, it will be over-written, that evidence is lost, and your client's defence (or equally the prosecutor's proof) has vanished. I've ended up making legal arguments in court that the failure of the CPS not to afford somebody CCTV evidence is so significant, that it would justify the case being thrown out – and the judges have agreed. What a waste of everyone's time, and of public money.

Joining the CPS or working as a defence lawyer are very different career choices. CPS staff might disagree, but I would say their workload is less, they have little engagement with individual clients, and there is more of a culture of 'do the hours you are paid for'. It is, however, possible to move around departments if you aren't enjoying your specific area, and it is much better paid, so there are positives.

When I was heading up a team of youth justice lawyers at a firm, I lost one of my best lawyers to the CPS as she was keen to buy a house, have children and generally enjoy a better way of life, which for those at the lower end of the defence profession is hard to envisage. By heading off to the CPS as a senior prosecutor, she was instantly on for a £15,000 pay rise and much easier hours, so sadly I couldn't blame her. However it doesn't seem good for the profession as a whole if people are making career choices driven by the need for an adequate salary, as opposed to finding the job that is right for them. I have now lost count of how many good defence solicitors have left the profession to obtain the work-life balance being a prosecutor offers. I take some comfort in the fact that there are now some more defence-minded prosecutors at least.

Age of Criminal Responsibility

The age of criminal responsibility in England, Wales and Northern Ireland is ten. That means if someone commits a crime at ten years old or above, they can be arrested, charged and prosecuted. If they commit a crime at nine years old or under, it is treated as though they were too young to take genuine responsibility for their actions, and cannot be charged. There will still be an intervention of sorts if it is felt necessary, but the offence will be handled more as a matter of welfare than a crime, with social services taking charge of any action that is needed.

The UK used to follow the common-law principle of *doli incapax* (from a Latin phrase meaning 'incapable of deceit'). This was the presumption in law that a child is incapable of forming the criminal intent to commit an offence, so even if the act committed would be considered a crime if carried out by an adult, a child is unable to go through the thought process needed to class it in such a way. In occasional, rare cases, even under the *doli incapax* principle it was held that sometimes children between the ages of ten and fourteen did have criminal responsibility, provided the prosecution could show that they were able to form the criminal intent rather than simply being mischievous or naughty.

But once the principle of *doli incapax* was scrapped in 1998, it became irrelevant whether a child of ten, eleven or older had a mental age of eight – their *biological* age was what mattered. Given our increased understanding of psychology and the way our minds work and develop, this felt like a step backwards, and as a country it makes our approach look antiquated in the eyes of others.

The UK has the lowest age of criminal responsibility in Europe. Scotland had originally been the lowest at just eight, but in December 2021 this was revised to twelve. Other European countries range across most of the teenage years, with France at thirteen, Germany at fourteen, Portugal at sixteen, and the highest in the world, Luxembourg, at eighteen. The United Nations Convention on the Rights of the Child recommends that the age of criminal responsibility should be twelve or more.

In my opinion and experience, it is very problematic to criminalize children as young as ten. Having them in custody, questioning them in the police station then making them stand in front of a judge risks giving them a deviant identity at a highly impressionable age. They are labelled before they have even come close to working out who they are, and it can end up becoming a self-fulfilling prophecy because of the impact that label has on shaping their future.

I strongly believe the current situation in this country is not appropriate, and while it is not as cut and dried as a simple number, if I had to put an age on it, I would say forget about ten – anyone under eighteen should not be put through a criminal process. Of course, sometimes children can be the perpetrators of serious violence, but on the whole there should be a welfare-based approach with a focus on therapeutic interventions to get the best results for all involved.

POINTERS FOR ANY YOUNG PERSON, OR THEIR PARENT, IF THEY ARE HEADED TO COURT

- Always send an adult with the child – decide who is most likely to be calm and supportive, the two most key attributes in court

- Attend on time

- Be prepared to wait, and bring phone chargers, a drink, etc., as there is often very little in the way of refreshment

- Arrange your own lawyer, someone you feel able to instruct and are confident in their abilities – and then trust them and let them do their job

- Provide your lawyer with as much information as possible and bring school records, diagnosis documents, healthcare plans ... anything that could help build a picture

- No matter how worried you are about it, turn up – a no-show will only make things much worse

CHAPTER 3

How Schools are Letting Our Children Down

Sasha was an artistic fourteen-year-old, who at home liked to create everything from sketches to homemade soap. So, when her craft, design and technology teacher asked the class to bring in an implement such as a spoon to school the next day so they could carve soap, Sasha was looking forward to showing off her skills. She brought in the craft knife she used in her spare time, and created some beautiful soaps in the lesson. Then, two days later during a random bag check, a teacher found the craft knife was still in her pencil case, and suddenly, she was seen as a risk.

At the time there was a concern about self-harm among her peers, but rather than either a) accept her explanation that she had forgotten the craft knife was there, and she would leave it at home that night, or b) deal with it as a safeguarding issue, take the sensitive approach and open up a conversation on self-harm, the school took the decision to involve the police.

Suddenly Sasha, who had an exemplary school record and was a well-regarded pupil by teachers and her peers, was being interviewed at the police station. I was contacted at this point, and arrived to find a distraught and frightened child, who couldn't understand why no one would believe her explanation. She was tearful, and afraid of saying the wrong thing.

Sasha was from a close-knit family, had lived a fairly sheltered life, and her parents until now had clearly had faith in the legal system, so were utterly appalled that their daughter was in a police interview for bringing a craft knife into school with the clear aim of using it to carve soap. I read a prepared statement for her in interview, and then the policeman began firing off questions. 'So, did you have this with you to self-harm?' he demanded, causing her to cry so hard we had to pause the interview. I was appalled at the insensitivity displayed by the officer.

Thankfully, the same day it was decided that no further action would be taken, and that was the end of it – at least as far as the police and the school were concerned. But I'm sure the impact on Sasha and her family went further. The whole thing was so unnecessary, and it was as though the situation was processed with no real thought about the impact on her well-being. Why did the school not just have a talk with her about the rules around bladed objects in school, sensitively check about self-harm, and then leave it there, rather than forcing the formal, and emotionally damaging, process of a police interview?

It is worth noting that had Sasha been stopped in the street after school and the police had come across the craft knife, the fact that she had it for an art class would most likely have been considered a reasonable excuse. The way the law works in this area is that if you are found in possession of a knife but can give a genuine, plausible reason for it, then there is a possibility you will not be charged – although who you are can also influence this. By this I mean an elderly lady with a knife and an apple in her bag (not that I can envisage someone like that being stopped and searched in the first place, but theoretically) who says, 'I have the knife with me to cut my apple when I'm ready to eat it', would be deemed to be giving a reasonable excuse. Or a chef in uniform on their way to work, who will clearly need to use a knife in the course of their employment, should also be fine.

However, a teenage boy with the same knife and apple, would be less likely to be believed, because of the prevalence of knife crime among young people. It can be a grey area to some degree, but I think in Sasha's case, her innocence would have been pretty clear from the outset.

One of my sons is very artistic and has lots of different craft knives and scissors to help with his hobbies, but as a result of this case I have been known to check his pencil case to make sure none of them are headed for school. The last thing I want is him having an experience like Sasha, or getting a criminal record for something he has taken to school for a totally innocent reason.

Sasha's school is not alone in the way they dealt with her case. The growing trend in recent years has been to refer to the police cases that would previously have been dealt with internally by the school, making school discipline a criminal matter. I'd like to look at the role of schools as far as the criminal justice system is concerned – and where I think they are going wrong.

Who is in charge of disciplining children at different points in the day can be a contentious conversation. How much does the responsibility lie with parents, even when children are away from home and out of their company? How much lies with teachers, police, the wider community? Everyone will have their own opinion on it, but even during the school day I don't think teachers should be expected to deal with everything – far from it; they have a tough enough job as it is. But it feels as though schools are deferring to the police more and more, when they should be dealing with issues through their own behaviour management policies.

So how did this shift come about? A fear of getting in trouble for not taking something seriously enough, which is self-preservation in a growing blame culture, is certainly one of the reasons. It feels safer, according to some teachers I have spoken with, to overreact as opposed to underreact. Then you can't be criticized for doing nothing.

I had one eleven-year-old client who had taken a small knife into school to impress her friends. It was her brother's camping knife and she had taken it from home to show it off in school. It seemed like it was more about misguided attention-seeking than actual threatening behaviour, but the teachers called the police, and she was interviewed under caution at the station and given an out-of-court disposal. It felt to me as if counselling might have been more beneficial to deal with her need to impress her friends in this way, and to redirect her ideas of what is acceptable and not. But she was really upset; the school had effectively alienated her by putting her in that situation at the police station, and any opportunity to speak to her about her motivation, and to work on that, was lost.

Equally though, it's understandable that, if your eleven-year-old child came home and said someone had brought a knife into school, you would be horrified, especially as, rightly or wrongly, the fear of knife crime is growing. The number of people killed with a knife in England and Wales between April 2021 and March 2022 was the highest on record for seventy-six years, and the greatest increase was among boys aged sixteen and seventeen. The causes of serious youth violence are complex but what is clear is that it will take a significant amount of investment in the community and therapeutic interventions to really tackle the issues.

No one would ever dispute that a child carrying a knife or other bladed object with the intention of harming, or threatening another, needs to be taken seriously and action needs to be taken to make the other pupils feel safe. I do, however, think a lot more emphasis needs to be put to the root cause of why this cycle is growing. If children are so scared they feel they need to have a knife for self-defence, for example, this is a sure indication that the issue had started long before the knife came onto the scene.

Every parent wants to feel that when they send their child off to school they will be safe, so a crackdown on knife crime has wide support. But there is a huge difference between dangerous blades carried with intent, and those that are so clearly the other end of the scale, and schools need to take on the management themselves in those cases, and stop automatically deferring to police. As with Sasha, some common sense needs to be applied. While the thought of knives in school may create fear in the minds of most parents, do the public really want to see a child arrested for having a craft knife in their pencil case, or using the wrong type of scissors in school?

Take fifteen-year-old Tina, who faced a similarly ridiculous accusation as Sasha did, but her experience sadly lasted much longer, partly due to the Covid-19 pandemic. Tina suffered eighteen months of angst. A string on her hair braids had broken and, during lunch break, she asked to borrow some scissors from a friend to cut them. After she had used the scissors, Tina sat chatting in the dinner hall, the scissors aimlessly dangling from her hand, only for a group of girls, who she had not been getting on with, to report her.

There had been no threatening words or actions, no suggestion that she was using, or intended to use the scissors for anything other than cutting her hair. But the school said they weren't the safety scissors she had use of in lessons – despite the fact there was nothing in their school policy to say you couldn't bring in a different kind of pair of scissors – and they referred the case to the Safer Schools Officer (SSO) attached to their school (see more about SSOs later in this chapter). Suddenly Tina was being called to the police station for interview, and being charged with possession of a bladed article or a sharply pointed article on school premises. I mean, that charge term alone inevitably conjures up frightening images for parents – you would hardly expect it to refer to something like this!

The Youth Offending Team said Tina could accept a conditional caution, and the initial lawyer they had working with her at the police station advised her to take it. In my opinion that advice was just a bit of a lazy: 'Oh, she's broken the rules, theoretically it can be argued what she did was against the law, so just accept the caution and be done with it.'

This lawyer hadn't engaged with who Tina was or tried to look into the situation. As someone who would have just been working for the set police station interview fee, it is maybe fair to say the financial incentive to delve into it further just wasn't there. Thankfully Tina's parents stood their ground and were so outraged at the idea she would have a criminal record for no good reason, they contacted me. I immediately thought it sounded like a case where this was a potential miscarriage of justice, and one where we could make a difference. Tina's parents didn't have a particularly positive opinion of the legal system, and they had an expectation that justice would not be served, but they were determined to give it their best shot and fight for it.

My first thought when hearing the circumstances, was, 'But did she actually break the law?' as to me it appeared that she hadn't. Talking it through with Tina and her parents, we decided to refuse the caution, so at the next interview we put forward a statement explaining the circumstances. The Safer Schools Officer (SSO) had clearly expected Tina to turn up and take the caution, and got quite angry and aggressive, repeatedly referring back to the advice of the previous lawyer. He seemed intent on saying the scissors had been waved in a threatening or aggressive manner, which my client adamantly disputed.

I advised Tina and her parents that I thought they had a good case, but to go to trial could be a long and stressful route. Instead, I said maybe we could look at accepting a community resolution, which meant she wouldn't be left with a criminal record as it is dealt with out of court (more on these in Chapter 12 on Different Sentencing Options). However, the Youth Offending Team, who I felt were being heavily influenced by the SSO, would not agree to this. So it was set for trial. Knowing just how farcical the whole thing seemed to be, I kept hoping the case would be dropped, but sixteen months on from the time of the incident, we appeared at the youth court to give initial representations; after that we had to wait another few months before the trial took place. At this point full disclosure meant we saw the statements, and none of the girls had claimed Tina was waving the scissors aggressively, so I had to wonder why the SSO had been so intent on pushing that narrative.

We had instructed a barrister on the case who does a lot of work with JfKL and is passionate about representing children, despite her day-to-day work being about much more serious matters at a Crown Court. She took it on as she thought it was so ridiculous, and kept emailing me to ask if 'this farce of a trial' was still going ahead. Tina had a psychological assessment during this time that confirmed how depressing the whole scenario was to her, how it was hanging over her head all the time and impacting on her self-esteem and identity, not to mention her education – this was all happening in the middle of her GCSEs.

In giving her thoughts at the end of the trial, the Chairwoman of the Bench commented on Tina's truthful and consistent manner, the fact that neither she nor her parents knew that scissors were a prohibited item, that the school recognized its error and changed its policy, and that she had a reasonable excuse. Unsurprisingly, Tina was acquitted, but I really had to ask, why was it ever in court?

It felt like classic over-policing of children. Rod Morgan, a former chair of the Youth Justice Board, once said: 'To meet crime targets, the police are picking low-hanging fruit – the lowest of which comprises juvenile group behaviour in schools, residential homes and public spaces, offences that could be dealt with informally, more effectively, speedily and cheaply, and in former times were.'

I absolutely feel that this is the truth: that to hit their targets in terms of number of arrests and charges, the police take the easy route by looking at children, which is one of the reasons why certain officers get particularly annoyed when defence solicitors like me don't just roll over and accept what they want to put on your client.

Alongside the court case, an ongoing battle had been running with the school, which had taken the decision to permanently exclude Tina over the incident. Luckily her determined parents decided to fight that too, challenging it on the grounds that the school's behaviour policy didn't specify that a pair of scissors was a prohibited item. Eventually the school had to reverse their decision, but what a potentially damaging set of circumstances, created in my opinion by the school not taking on the responsibility of managing its pupils in the way it should. If there was one good thing that came out of it all, it was that Tina's interest in the legal system had been piqued, and she went on to university to study law.

There is an unmistakable element of box-ticking going on within all these cases, too. It is concerning that I seem to be regularly attending police stations to assist a growing number of children who are called in for what are misguided or badly-thought-out choices, but ultimately prove to be harmless. The system means that everyone from teachers to police officers have to follow the rule book so as not to potentially get themselves into trouble. However, while covering for themselves, the result means children like Harry have to bear the brunt.

One Saturday Harry had been playing football and was walking home past his old primary school with a friend when they saw it was open. Harry had enjoyed a very positive experience there, and missed it, so was pleased at the chance to show his new friend where his classroom had been, see if there were any old teachers around he could say hi to, and I guess he just generally wanted to reminisce. The boys respectfully took off their boots so as not to traipse mud around the building, left them by the school's front door, and wandered through. They bumped into Harry's former PE teacher and had a chat with him, but then further on when they opened another door, it triggered an alarm. After that, protocol took over from common sense. The headteacher had to explain what happened to the alarm company. The alarm company then reported it as a break-in to the police for insurance purposes. And before you know it, the boys were hauled in for interview under suspicion of burglary. Everyone was following the steps their job instructed them to do, but I doubt anyone involved actually thought these children should be arrested.

The fact that these two boys were considerate enough to leave their boots by the door and stopped for a chat with a teacher should have been a pretty good indicator that burglary wasn't exactly at the forefront of their minds. In reality, what Harry needed was a reminder from his parents that, while the school might have felt like a place he was free to roam in for four years, that was no longer the case; and his friend should maybe be talked to about simply following the other boy's lead. But suddenly it had become a protracted and intimidating process and I was brought in to advise the children on their defences. Thankfully, the case was dropped, but you must be reading this wondering if the police and I spend our days on farcical cases!

Safer for Whom?

The arrival of police officers actually based in schools, the Safer Schools Officers (SSOs), has taken police involvement with children to a whole new level. SSOs deal with anything from being the point of contact for teachers, to handling the aftermath of a playground fight. It is almost as though schools are subcontracting out behaviour management.

As far as I am concerned, the idea of having police officers in schools is hugely problematic. The biggest issues we have found with it are:

- Children being criminalized in situations where they previously wouldn't have been

- The issues caused by the school investigation preceding a police investigation, from the collection of evidence to a child's rights – is it a school process, or a criminal justice process?

- The negative perception children develop towards police officers after they have been stationed in schools

In 2021 there were 683 police SSOs in schools across the country, in particular in more deprived, inner city areas. By the start of 2023 this had risen by 43 per cent to 979, with plans to increase this number. According to the most recent information gathered by the Runnymede Trust, these officers were more likely to be based in schools with higher numbers of children on free school meals, and often with higher numbers of black pupils.

Previously, with most issues that occurred in school, the starting point would be teachers working out how they want to resolve an issue. Now anything that can be seen to even have a whiff of illegality to it gets referred to SSOs, it is escalated to a legal matter, and children are being criminalized. Police should only be brought in when necessary, not be there as a constant presence becoming involved at the most minute level – which, inevitably, is what ends up happening.

Nor is the public's perception of the move a particularly positive one. You only have to put it into Google, and instantly the headlines from recent years come up:

- 'Petrified boy, 12, spoken to by a police officer over a false claim of cookie theft'

- 'Having police in school is emblematic of a society heading in the wrong direction'

- 'Concerns raised over role of Met police in schools'

Interestingly enough, many officers I have spoken to have also expressed an annoyance at being posted at schools, feeling they are wasting their time on issues that the school should be dealing with. I've been called out to incidents several times where an officer will say: 'I don't know why we are here. If your client says nothing, we will take no further action.'

But ultimately, the child still had to go through the process, and the children we speak to are developing a greater negative perception of the police, some of which is thanks to an experience they have had in school. There are children who would never have come to the attention of the courts before but now, because of the school choosing to use the officer route, they are within the system, often feeling they are there unfairly, and so their perception of justice is impacted.

Dr Remi Joseph-Salisbury is Reader in Sociology at the University of Manchester. In a newspaper article in 2021 he wrote:

> School-based police are perhaps the ultimate signal of a society's low expectations for young people. The message they transmit is an incredibly harmful one: what is expected of young people is not 'academic success', but criminality. Surely, this is not the aspirational culture we want to create in our schools.
>
> Whether it's stigmatizing schools, creating a climate of fear and hostility, making young people feel unsafe or feeding a school-to-prison pipeline, there are many issues to suggest that school-based police are emblematic of a society heading in the wrong direction.

Unfortunately, I have to agree with him that this seems to be exactly the message being sent out to our young people. Dr Joseph-Salisbury is part of a coalition, the Kids of Colour project, that in 2020 launched a No Police in Schools campaign, focused on concern at the increased police presence in schools in Greater Manchester and beyond. Their research resulted in a report called 'Decriminalize the Classroom: A Community Response to Police in Greater Manchester's Schools', which flagged up a lot of negative thoughts and feelings around the issue from young people.

In addition, the race equality think tank Runnymede Trust, in their 2023 report 'Over-policed and under-protected', found that the presence of police in schools resulted in an escalation of minor disciplinary issues into criminal justice issues, particularly for those from minority groups.

What was interesting was the praise that the 'Decriminalize the Classroom' report received from teachers. The National Education Union in the Greater Manchester region passed a motion for no police in schools, and many of its members threw their support behind the campaign. So, if teachers themselves aren't in favour of these Safer School Officers – and neither are pupils or officers – what are we doing?

I spoke to one teacher in a school with an SSO who told me that teachers are actively working against the SSO, trying to make sure he or she doesn't get wind of an issue. Instead, teachers try to deal with what is behind the issue themselves to stop the potential criminalization of children.

Both the Metropolitan Police and Avon and Somerset Police faced legal challenges, in which they had to review police in schools on the basis that their presence had a disproportionately negative effect on pupils from black and ethnic minority backgrounds, and those with special education needs and disabilities. The thinking was that the presence of police in schools could cause pupils to be drawn into the criminal justice system unnecessarily. As a result, both forces agreed to carry out further assessments to find out if that was the case, and to look into the roles that SSOs play, and the challenges were dropped.

Who Investigates, and How?

So, there are many reasons why police officers in schools are not a good idea. Another problem with deferring to the police in a school is that it creates a situation in which the school's role is very unclear. After all, when it is clear that a genuine criminal offence has occurred, schools should not be taking on the role of police in the investigation.

For example, there can be cases when the school is not fully managing the child's behaviour, but equally isn't always happy to completely hand the situation over, so the school can end up sitting in the middle, which is dangerous territory. What I mean by that, is that in their behaviour policies, schools have the right to take statements from children when an incident has occurred, to gather more information, then to consider the appropriate action to take. But what is happening is they are doing the first part, then passing that information on to officers, who then start the formal process. However, what has happened *informally* could potentially impede the formal investigation. There are several ways this can happen, for example, a teacher might not understand what evidence needs to be preserved and what doesn't, and may omit to do something that an officer would do, such as look at a mobile phone.

However, more importantly, teachers simply aren't trained in taking statements in the way that police officers are. There are all sorts of rules and guidance around interviewing, laid out in the Police and Criminal Evidence Act (PACE) from 1984 that gives codes of practice, regulates police powers and protects public rights. This ensures an officer doesn't lead a person being interviewed down a certain route, or put words into their mouth. A teacher may not even realize they are doing this.

The children don't have any of the protections that would be in place during a police interview: they aren't told their rights and don't understand that what they are saying can have a negative impact on the evidence. When the police carry out questioning in school, they are still required to act under PACE – although the school setting allows for a more relaxed approach.

A child also thinks very differently when talking to a teacher than he or she would when talking to a police officer – children's witness statements are regularly entirely different to what they initially said at school, as at that point they are just thinking about whether they are going to get detention. I've also had situations in which one child says something then, as others want to be part of the drama, they all join in and say the same thing. This lack of clarity around the process causes so many issues, and is something of great concern to me for the key role it is playing in how the system is failing. Once an incident becomes a legal proceeding, or it looks as if there's a chance of it heading that way, the school can't keep trying to play a part in the situation. If they are going to get an officer involved, it definitely isn't their place to do any kind of investigating themselves. They need to handle it internally or hand it over completely.

A Safe Place for Children?

A well-known case that encapsulates my feelings about police being brought into school is the humiliating strip-search of Child Q, who you may have read about in the news. She was a fifteen-year-old black girl, and in December 2020 teachers contacted police, concerned that she might have cannabis in her possession. Two female officers came to the school, took Child Q out of an exam, and carried out a full strip-search in the medical room, even insisting she remove her sanitary towel. Her parents weren't contacted and no appropriate adult was present, with teachers waiting outside the room. All of this blatantly goes against PACE guidance on how searches should be carried out.

The girl was strongly affected by the experience, and sought counselling. Her family approached us and one of our Education solicitors took on her case to raise as a complaint against the school. We also referred her to another legal firm to take action against the police, as this isn't an area we cover. In a safeguarding report by the City and Hackney Safeguarding Children Partnership, the search was described as traumatic and disproportionate, and the report stated that racism was 'likely to have been an influencing factor'. It pointed towards the likelihood of 'adultification bias', where a black child is seen as being older and less vulnerable than their white peers. Metropolitan Police figures show that 650 children were strip-searched by that force alone between 2018 and 2020, with the figure at nearly one a day in 2020, despite much of that year being dominated by the pandemic and lockdowns. In 23 per cent of the cases, according to the data gathered by the Children's Commissioner for England, an appropriate adult was not present.

The case of Child Q really horrified me – that this happened to her at all is bad enough, but that it was allowed to happen in a place where safeguarding is meant to be paramount is unbelievable. Thankfully, it has caused outrage among many other members of society too, and there are a number of ongoing campaigns as a result, that I sincerely hope lead to change.

For me school was a sanctuary, and I had many teachers over the years whose flexible approach to 'pastoral care' provided me with support when I most needed it. For example, my French exchange trip was mysteriously paid for when we struggled to make the payments, or there would be extra check-ins, without actually exposing to others that things were not plain sailing for me at home. I simply can't imagine my teachers at that time calling in the police for any of the cases discussed throughout this chapter. Any incident would have been dealt with directly and compassionately. That is how I feel it should be in all schools – they should be a place of safety, where relationships between teachers and children are not compromised by criminal investigations.

School Exclusions

While not theoretically a part of criminal law, I want to take a moment to address school exclusions, as there is unfortunately a direct correlation between children who are excluded from school and those who become involved in the criminal justice system. Eight out of every ten children in custody have been excluded from school, so there is a strong argument for looking long and hard at how and why exclusions happen, and seeing what can be done to change that. Sometimes a child is already in the criminal system and then gets excluded, or it might happen at the same time, but exclusion is far too frequently the first step that almost ensures a child's life is going to head on a downward trajectory.

We saw a rise in exclusions in the months following the return to schools after the Covid-19 lockdowns. The indications were that the rise tied in with poor mental health, perhaps partly caused by the lack of connection with schools and other students. My concern is that exclusions are a way of managing challenging behaviour by effectively shoving it under the carpet. The school makes that child someone else's responsibility, instead of getting to the bottom of the problem and supporting the child to cope or adapt.

I fully understand why a teacher wouldn't want a disruptive pupil in their class. They are trying to teach say thirty students, and can't afford to spend half their time dealing with one student. Nor is it fair on the rest of the room. This tends to be the main reason a school will give for excluding a child. But to flip it on its head, rather than putting the responsibility on the child, it would be fair to say that often the pupil's needs are not being met by the school. Are they getting the support to deal with any outside factors that might be impacting on them and causing them to behave in this way?

More commonly, the pupil might be dealing with an undiagnosed mental health issue, special educational need or disability. Shockingly, SEND children – those with Special Educational Needs and Disabilities – are six times more likely to be excluded from school than their peers. They may have attention deficit hyperactivity disorder (ADHD), autism or social communication issues, all of which can manifest themselves as 'bad behaviour' in a school setting. It is incredible how many children I deal with in the criminal justice system who, within a very short time of meeting them, give me a sense that there is an undiagnosed neurodiversity issue. Talking to their parents and hearing more about their behaviour at home and school, it becomes even more clear, and yet no one in their educational setting has followed it up before.

Guidance for schools, especially those that might be considering exclusion, is to investigate whether disruptive behaviour may be as a result of an unmet need, perhaps caused by an undiagnosed special educational need or disability, then to act on what they find. Once diagnosed, the local authority has a duty to provide additional resources to the school for that child, allowing the teacher to hopefully continue their job, and for the child to remain in mainstream education with their peers.

The sticking point occurs when either the teacher isn't au fait with SEND children, and doesn't spot that might be the problem, or they do realize what is happening and try to refer them for a diagnosis, only to find that the current waiting list for adolescent and youth mental health appointments is a year to eighteen months. Without that diagnosis and a statement of special educational needs, even a teacher who is aware of the situation has their hands tied. So in the meantime the child's behaviour and associated issues may continue, he or she gets caught up in an escalating series of sanctions, and it leads to permanent exclusion.

You've got to ask what message we are giving to so many of these children, and in my experience, they often feel they are being abandoned and written off.

The school exclusion process itself is quite complex, and seems to be weighted in favour of the school. There will be a hearing with the child, their parents, the school governors, a representative of the local authority if requested, and often the headteacher. Everyone is allowed to say their bit, although the sense is often that the governors just sign off on the headteacher's decision. Parents aren't entitled to legal representation, unless they pay for it, which feels flawed from the outset. It is quite a formal and complicated hearing, and parents often have to argue cases – some involving really complex legal principles – themselves, if they want to feel as if they have a voice in the process at all. Does that really seem fair? As a result, a number of charities now provide free advocacy or representation at school exclusion hearings. Up until August 2023, JfKL had an education team who focused on this area, however due to funding constraints we have had to transfer this project to Coram Children's Legal Centre, where it continues to thrive.

It is not just the parents that require support during the case. Equally, children we work with often say that they feel they have had no part to play in the decisions being made about them. They feel that they are on the periphery of the decision-making, not allowed to participate directly in the hearing or able to find a way to get their voice heard. That is something that JfKL would like to see changed, and is one of the aspects the School Exclusions project at Coram continues to tackle through the School Exclusion Campaign, which is led by young people impacted by exclusion.

Frustratingly, children or their parents don't have the right to appeal a school exclusion. There is an Independent Review Panel (IRP) that can make comments and recommendations, but unfortunately they don't have any real power. So for example, if the review panel thought the school had been too heavy handed, they could not make them reverse the decision, but can only make recommendations that the pupil is reinstated. Statistics suggest that schools aren't too keen on listening to the IRP however, with only 20 per cent of students being offered a chance to return to the school off the back of the IRP advice. A child either ends up with nowhere to go, and is just left hanging around with other excluded kids from their area or with older youths who have left education, or they are sent to a pupil referral unit (PRU).

PRUs are set up specifically for children who can't attend mainstream education for a variety of reasons, but exclusion tends to be the main cause. Sometimes publicly and sometimes privately run, they offer smaller timetables, fewer subjects, and around half the number of GCSEs that would be on offer in a mainstream school. So for a child who did have a genuinely good chance of succeeding in education, a move to a PRU makes it much harder. This is perhaps reflected in statistics from 2020 that showed 96 per cent of PRU pupils failed English and Maths GCSEs.

There is also the issue that, unfortunately, PRUs can be a breeding ground for child criminal exploitation. Time and again it feels very much like this is a group of invisible children, excluded from mainstream services and society.

What is the Alternative?

Some schools have begun their own onsite exclusion units and I am interested to see how these work out. The idea is that these young people still come under the mainstream umbrella, so they can access all subjects, but are essentially in another unit outside the mainstream setting, to prevent disruption to other pupils while their needs are met.

Even putting aside the welfare of the children involved, the maths would suggest that the financially smarter move is to put more funding into supporting schools to find ways to keep the children in mainstream education. Excluding a child from school and instead putting them through a pupil referral unit costs ten times more than keeping them in a school. Then we need to factor in that the chance of them ending up in prison becomes much higher, and the cost of keeping a young person in prison is around £30,000 to £50,000 a year. Add the financial argument to an understanding of what is best for the welfare of the children, and in my mind a move towards a zero expulsion system is the only sensible decision.

WHAT TO DO IF YOUR CHILD IS FACING EXCLUSION

There are a number of steps you can and should take if this situation arises.

- See if the school will have an initial meeting with you to discuss options, and if there is a way the situation can be dealt with without things escalating

- Speak to a charity that helps with school exclusion and get some legal advice or representation

- Look to the IRP if the decision doesn't go your way

USEFUL CONTACTS

Some good charities to contact for help with school exclusion and for representation are:

- School Exclusions Hub www.schoolexclusionshub.org.uk/

- Communities Empowerment Network info@cenlive.org 0207 733 0292

- No More Exclusions www.nomoreexclusions.com

- School Exclusion project at City University schoolexclusionsproject@cityac.uk

Other universities have pro bono projects as well, so it is worth checking out your local ones

CHAPTER 4

Choose Your Friends Carefully

Imagine your child is hanging around with a group of friends in the local park on a Saturday afternoon. They're chatting, taking pictures, messing around on the skateboard ramp, and generally just relaxing as teenagers do. Then one of the boys, bored and showing off, starts saying he is going to steal a phone from another boy he can see walking nearby. Your child isn't listening, busy chatting with another friend, and doesn't really know what is happening, until the boy who has now snatched the phone is sprinting off across the park, laughing. Your son isn't impressed, but doesn't feel he can say much, and no one else is really reacting, so at the first chance he and another friend leave the group and head home.

That evening, there is a knock at your door, and your child is arrested on suspicion of robbery. Your son tells you and the police an honest account of what happened, but it isn't good enough – the victim has described your child as being there when the phone was stolen; the whole group is guilty by association. Your son, and the rest of the group of friends, are charged with robbery under the doctrine of joint enterprise.

Maybe that sounds far-fetched, but I can promise you, it is

not. In the eyes of the law, what your peer group does in your presence can have a huge impact on your own dealings with the police and the courts. The doctrine of joint enterprise implies that we are all responsible for what people around us do. And yet mention the phrase 'joint enterprise' to most people, and they think it is a rarely used charge that only refers to a situation in which one of two people must have committed a serious crime, there is no conclusive evidence which of them it was, and they both blame each other, or deny it, so they both face the same sentence.

The reality is very different.

The Crown Prosecution Service describes joint enterprise as follows:

> Where two or more persons are involved in
> an offence, the parties to the offence may be
> principals (D1) or secondary parties (accessories)
> (D2). A principal is one who carries out the
> substantive offence i.e. the unlawful act and has
> an unlawful intent. If two or more persons do so,
> they are joint principals … A secondary party
> is one who aids, abets, counsels or procures
> (commonly referred to as assists or encourages)
> D1 to commit the substantive offence.

Putting it simply, joint enterprise means a person can be jointly convicted of the crime carried out by another person if the court decides they assisted or encouraged the other person to commit that crime. So even if only one person has been directly involved in a crime, other people who were not the one striking the fatal blow or snatching the phone can be held responsible. There are varying degrees of involvement, from encouraging the main perpetrator, to carrying out a physical attack in some way, to just being there and not doing anything to actively prevent the crime being committed or firmly withdrawing from it. In all those situations, joint enterprise is a means of charging that can be applied. It is a complex area of law with many factors to be considered, however the aim of this book is to highlight the legal issues that are most likely to impact children.

Over the years, joint enterprise has become increasingly controversial, particularly for its use in trials involving children and young people, where it was commonly applied. However, it doesn't take into account a number of factors.

At JfKL we believe there are a couple of major oversights that arise with joint enterprise charges when it comes to children:

- Their brain development and foresight
- The pack mentality and peer group pressure

Adolescent Brain Development and the Issue of Foresight

The doctrine of joint enterprise has evolved somewhat following a legal challenge in a case called *Jogee* (see later in this chapter). The court concluded in the *Jogee* case that the law had been interpreted incorrectly for many years as courts had been equating a person's ability to foresee that a crime may happen, with intent. Instead, what someone should have reasonably foreseen should just be *part* of the evidence the CPS can use to show that a person intended to assist or encourage another to commit the crime.

The idea that a person was able to foresee that someone they were with was likely to commit an offence, is often a key feature in joint enterprise cases. But my argument would be that a child simply does not have the same ability to predict actions or events, or understand the consequences of them, in a way that an adult would.

Let's say that a young person has started carrying a knife. Most adults would foresee that there is a much higher chance that they could cause serious harm, and end up with a grievous bodily harm charge, or worse. An adolescent brain often genuinely has trouble foreseeing and avoiding situations which have the potential to escalate, and so the young person doesn't tend to extricate themselves at a time when an adult would. This applies to both the person with the knife, and any friend who was with them at the time of an incident.

I think it is worth pausing here and looking at a teenage brain in a bit more detail. We all joke: 'Who knows what goes on inside their brains?' and the reality is, not as much study as you might think had been done in this area until recent years. One fascinating aspect that has emerged is that this area of teenage behaviour is not down to hormones, as might have been previously thought, but actual physical brain development.

The areas of the brain known as the frontal lobes and prefrontal cortex are the parts that control impulses, regulate aggression, calm emotions, encourage consequential and abstract thinking, and allow reasoned, logical and rational decision-making processes. However, they are the slowest areas of the brain to develop during the adolescent years. Instead teenagers rely on the area of the brain that is associated with reward, emotional responses and gut reactions. Sounds about right, for much of the behaviour we associate with teenagers on a day-to-day basis, doesn't it?

Sarah-Jayne Blakemore, Professor of Psychology at Cambridge University, has spent the last twenty years focusing on adolescent brain development, and has made many interesting observations. She looks at the areas that influence risk-taking, decision-making, emotional regulation, self-awareness and social understanding. These are fascinating areas for any parent to know more about in their child, and for me they can be very relevant when related to a child's likelihood of ending up in the criminal legal system. Professor Blakemore and her team have studied the increase and decrease in white and grey matter in young brains, and concluded that while young people reach maturity at different stages, the average age is about twenty-five years old – not eighteen, as the law sees it.

Her research has gone a long way to proving that children and teens really don't have the same ability to predict events, or understand the consequences of their own and other's actions, in the way most adults do. Think of the things that any one of us did as teenagers that now seem astounding: why did I never think doing *that* would lead to *that*?

I see it with my teenage son right now. I'm at the stage when I am working towards giving him more freedom, but I still have to give him a whole host of instructions to account for the lack of consequential thinking. So, if he is going to a crowded event, I'd say: 'Keep your phone out of sight; stick in the family-friendly areas; keep your wallet in a zipped pocket.' The perception of other people's intentions just isn't there either, so playing out the possible consequences becomes even harder. A lot of my clients just haven't really thought about what someone else might do.

While part of it is down to science, there is also a degree of life experience that goes into this development too – which may be one of the reasons why I seemed to mature and have fairly good foresight in my teenage years at a younger age than most.

Back in my role with the Youth Offending Team, a lot of my work with somebody after their case had finished would be looking back over what had happened and discussing what they had been thinking at different points, the decisions they made and why, and what might have happened if they had made a different decision. At that point, all my work would aim to make them see how consequences can play out.

Pack Mentality

Then there is the issue of pack mentality. When it comes to peer influence, Professor Blakemore says:

> Adolescents are more likely to take risks, such as engaging in reckless behaviour and experimenting with drugs, alcohol and cigarettes, when they are with their friends than when alone. Many studies have shown that peer influence is a particularly strong determinant of behaviour in adolescence.
>
> Adolescents are hypersensitive to social evaluation and are driven to impress their peers and seek their approval.

We regularly use Professor Blakemore's thoughts and findings as part of our evidence in court. They give an insight, in a clear, factual way that we hope judges and juries will respond to, into why we can't necessarily judge an adolescent's behaviour with the same set of societal expectations as we can an adult's.

Professor Blakemore continues:

> We have proposed that adolescents are especially motivated by a need to be included in their social group and a desire to avoid social exclusion. As such, peer influence (and the drive to avoid social risk) is a major determinant of adolescent behaviour. Specifically, choosing not to take part in a risky behaviour in which one's friends are engaged is a significant risk for an adolescent. Indeed, this might be considered more risky than the health risks or legal risks of the behaviours that their friends are engaging in because it increases the threat of social exclusion. In other words, choosing to say no to friends might be a more risky option for an adolescent than going along with the risky behaviour their friends are engaging in.

She gives the example of a teenage boy who is offered an illegal drug by his friends, who are all taking the drug. To his mind, Professor Blakemore explains, it might be riskier to decline the drug and potentially ostracize himself from his peers, than to go along with them and accept the drug. It goes some way to explaining why deciding to engage in risky behaviours such as smoking or binge drinking when in a peer group setting, while not being an objectively 'good' decision, might not necessarily be an irrational choice for adolescents when these behaviours are valued by the peer group. Professor Blakemore reasons that if engaging in behaviours, no matter how risky, increases their social status and reduces their chance of rejection, this may be especially important for adolescents.

This same trait of risky behaviour to impress peers can be seen in data on young drivers put together in recent years by the American Automobile Association Foundation. Unfortunately, a need to impress their peers with riskier driving seems to be an ongoing issue – a teenager's risk of death increases by 44 per cent with one teenage passenger, and quadruples with three or more teenage passengers. It implies that a young person's propensity to take on a different style of driving rises when they have passengers. They become notably more reckless if they think that is what their peers approve of.

Making allowances for pack mentality is a tricky one to get people on board with, as it can be quite a horrible trait to witness, with at times, some very unpleasant consequences. But try and imagine it closer to home and it makes more sense: we all have that daughter, or nephew, or son's friend, who we describe as 'easily-led' and worry that they will end up in trouble by just copying their friends. Taking that individual approach and imagining them getting caught in crime because of pack mentality, makes it a little easier to understand.

Professor Blakemore goes on to say that reporting a friend to the authorities, or 'snitching', would have the opposite social impact by heightening the young person's risk of social rejection. Avoiding that rejection might be of greater value to an adolescent brain than correcting a wrongdoing by another.

Lack of Foresight + Peer Pressure = A Recipe for Disaster

Add these two things together for young people, and in many ways it really is a recipe for disaster, being cooked up for many young people. The ability to see what is going to happen, and then have the strength of character to stop it, or remove yourself from the situation, is just so hard. I am forever hammering it home to my son: 'At the first sign of trouble, you leave. Anyone even talks about doing something you know isn't right, you get yourself out of there.' It is the safest thing they can do and keeps the message simple for a young person.

The Adjustments That Have Been Made to the Law

Prior to 2015, we were seeing huge groups of young people hauled into the police station or up in court together, charged as though they were one living, breathing, organism. It was common to see trials at the Old Bailey with ten, twelve, fifteen children all in the dock, charged with a stabbing or murder.

You might remember the tragic murder in Victoria Station in London in 2013 of a fifteen-year-old boy called Sofyen

Belamouadden. The death happened as a result of a falling out between children from two rival schools, and a planned attack during rush hour.

I was called in to deal with several clients who had been picked up around the area and taken to Charing Cross Police Station. The upstairs floor of the station, which wasn't normally open, had been turned into what can only be described as a processing factory, to work through all the children who had been arrested, carry out interviews, and do identification captures. Identification captures are basically the modern-day equivalent of an in-person identity parade, in which a digital image of the person might be used as part of a series of pictures for witnesses to check if they can pick out people they have seen at the incident.

One client in particular sticks in my head from that day, as he was one of the children who was taken to the station, but didn't know who had been killed. He was overwhelmed with panic by the time I got to him. He had been present when the incident had all kicked off, had been chased, and was understandably terrified and ran away. In my initial conversation with him he was convinced that one of his friends was the murder victim, and kept asking me to check. I asked the officer for disclosure, so I could break it to my client, but he wouldn't tell me who the victim was, determined to withhold it until during the interview. Sure enough, my client's concerns were founded and the victim was one of his friends. It was such a traumatic way for him to find out the news: to have this officer sensationally reveal it in the middle of the interview, as though hoping for some kind of revelation. My client wasn't charged, but I was angry at the way it had been handled – as though every child the police had rounded up was one and the same. Rather than an insensitive grilling and being treated like a defendant, my client should have been getting counselling or support to help him deal with what had happened, the senseless death of a friend.

There was a lot of coverage at the time – partly because girls were also being arrested, which always garners more press interest – and while it was hard to tell the exact number of children at the station as they were spread between rooms, it was evident there were a lot. There was an attitude from the start that any child in the vicinity was pretty much guilty by association, and even from those first hours it was clear this was going to be handled through joint enterprise.

In the end, twenty defendants were charged, and ended up in court across multiple linked trials, with eight eventually convicted of the killing.

At JfKL we had become increasingly uncomfortable over the years about the growing number of young people convicted under the joint enterprise law, as it didn't show any acknowledgment of each of those involved in a trial as individuals, but more as one group convicted en masse. So, in 2011, we started researching the issue, and made a submission to the House of Commons Justice Committee, flagging up our concerns. Then, in October 2015, we intervened in the Supreme Court case of *Jogee* (which I mentioned earlier as involving a challenge to the idea of joint enterprise). An intervention means that the court has given permission to third parties, who aren't acting for the defendant or prosecutor, to submit evidence which could be helpful to the judges in reaching an informed decision.

In this case, Jogee had been present when his friend and another man had been involved in an angry exchange, and shouted words of encouragement to his friend, who stabbed and killed the other man. The main point of contention was around foresight, and whether his words of encouragement meant that Jogee had intended his friend to commit murder, and whether he should face the same conviction.

In this situation the defendant – Jogee – was an adult, but we felt that the joint enterprise issue has such a disproportionate impact on young people, that intervening would help with the issue across all age groups. Our evidence to the court included the research from Professor Blakemore and the other academics at Cambridge University, demonstrating that young people often haven't yet gone through the necessary cognitive development to foresee how situations would unfold. Therefore, they may have genuine difficulties in avoiding situations that have the potential to escalate. This is particularly true of young people with special educational needs and disabilities.

Evidence was also given by campaigners from Joint Enterprise Not Guilty by Association, Jengba is a grassroots campaign run by volunteers, many of whom are family members whose loved ones have been convicted as a result of joint enterprise. They are very active in lobbying and campaigning around the cause and we have worked on cases together previously.

As I touched on earlier, the Supreme Court ruled that the joint enterprise law had been wrongly interpreted for the last thirty years, and clarified that foresight alone is not enough to confirm intention. I don't think the UK Supreme Court considered the issue closely enough in terms of young people, but the ruling felt like a start, and as a result, we have seen quite a change when it comes to murder cases. Thankfully, the days of twenty defendants up in court together seems to be a thing of the past.

Unfortunately, however, it seems to have made very little retrospective difference for people sentenced under joint enterprise before 2015. Quite a few people have looked at appealing their sentences off the back of this ruling, and we have represented some of these, but I can think of only one person who has successfully overturned their conviction. Sadly, it seems the courts are only prepared to take this change on board going forward. I believe there are many young people sitting in prison on joint enterprise charges who probably have good grounds to challenge their convictions, but won't be able to, even though the outcome would have potentially been different for them were the trial to happen today.

Significantly, joint enterprise is still widely used by police and the CPS when charging people in cases other than murder. It is particularly common with street robberies, and trying to separate out children in these situations, and avoid them being criminalized is difficult, so all I can advise is an increased awareness.

Going back to the mobile phone example at the start of this chapter, this is a scenario we see time and again, and when a confused young person is telling me, 'But it wasn't me,' I still have to explain why they have been charged with robbery. Even if they weren't comfortable with their friend's behaviour, their mere presence, demeanour, stance, build … *any* of it can unintentionally add to the intimidation of the victim. They look at the person demanding the phone, see four others behind him, and feel they have no choice but to hand it over. It is very hard to argue in court that your client's presence wasn't implicit in the offence, when you have a witness statement from a young person saying, 'I didn't know what else to do, there were lots of them, and I was scared.'

My client would have had to take some very deliberate action to show that they didn't agree with what was happening – such as telling their friend to stop, or trying to get them to hand the phone back – for it to stand up in court as a possible defence against joint enterprise.

So many children get swept up in these cases. It is very hard to have to explain to a child and their parents why sometimes it might be simpler to make admissions and accept an out-of-court disposal, if it is the first time they have been arrested, than to take it to trial. The way they see it is that they haven't done anything wrong, and I have to have some very frank conversations about the risks they would be taking in going to court as, in the eyes of the law, their presence was part and parcel of the crime. The choice of whether to risk a trial or not is entirely theirs, and I would not influence someone to make a decision one way or the other. My job is just to make sure they are aware of all the possible options and outcomes. It is tough to deal with, though, as if they choose to go to trial they may have a conviction for robbery on their record, which can cover anything from being nearby when their friend took money from someone, through to an armed robbery. Robbery covers anything that is theft with force, whether that is violence, threats or intimidation.

I can only emphasize the importance of being aware of the kind of company your child keeps, and doing all you can to encourage them to know their own mind, and, if they don't feel capable of preventing any issues that they can see arising, to remove themselves from the situation at the earliest opportunity.

In December 2023, Kim Johnson, Labour MP for Liverpool Riverside, presented her private members bill, The Joint Enterprise (Significant Contribution) Bill, with the aim of amending the Accessories and Abettors Act (1861) to provide that only a person who directly commits or who makes a significant contribution to the commission of an offence may be held criminally liable. It had its second reading in Parliament in early February 2024 and was adjourned until later in the year. This change could make an important difference in joint enterprise cases going forward.

Not Just For Kids Law ...

Despite the name of our organization, we represent quite a few people over the age of eighteen. For the reasons discussed earlier about adolescent brain development, the mental age of some of our clients who are legally young adults might still be like that of a thirteen- or fourteen-year-old, so we feel that it is only right to support them until their brains have reached mental maturity. There is a great deal of case law that says eighteen should not be such a cut-and-dried switch in how a person is treated in court, and there has been quite a movement to encourage courts to treat young adults differently. Thankfully, the courts are becoming aware of it, and are perhaps starting to consider it in the way the trial is handled. But ultimately the sentencing guidelines do instantly change at eighteen, and there is no sign of that being adjusted. From our side though, we prepare for the trials of young adults in much the same way as any other case.

This age disparity is also recognized within the care system, where people can be looked after by social services up until the age of twenty-five if they are in full-time education or training. The Leaving Care guidelines mean that after the age of twenty-five the young person is no longer housed in a care home, but is moved to semi-independent living, then independent living, then social housing, and is supported along the way. We follow these same parameters, and have done lots of research into what seems to be the appropriate level of support, so our general rule of thumb is we will take on a new client up to the age of twenty-one, if we feel their case fits with the kind of work we do. If they are an existing client, we will work with them until they are twenty-five.

WHERE TO GET HELP

Joint Enterprise Not Guilty by Association (JENGbA) have a website www.jointenterprise.co, are very active on social media, or you can drop them an email at jointenterpriseinfo@gmail.com

CHAPTER 5

Social Media, Sex and the Law

I doubt there is one parent reading this who won't have struggled to get their head around social media over recent years, and how exactly to influence, police, or engage with their child's use of it. This new method of communication has proven to be an absolute minefield since its arrival, but while this is the case for all of society, in particular it seems to be a real recipe for disaster for children.

I'm not a big advocate of using social media, especially when it comes to young people, as I think the negative impact it has outweighs the positive aspects. It can have real repercussions on everything from their mental health and well-being, to their perception of what beauty and success looks like. Children are especially vulnerable to this around the ages of eleven to thirteen, when they are trying to form their sense of self.

Then there is the aspect of addiction, as a person gets a dopamine hit every time they receive positive reactions such as 'likes' – how incredibly damaging must that be, to be exposed to something that makes you addicted to measuring your self-worth in such a way?

My eldest son was thirteen before I let him have a mobile phone, and I'm keen to keep him off most social media for as long as possible, although I had a daily debate with my son about my decision not to let him have Snapchat. I finally conceded just before his fifteenth birthday. I don't want my children to become obsessed with who everyone else is, when they need to focus on working out who *they* are.

But those are my own feelings towards social media – I'm no expert in the field, and there are many in-depth studies out there advocating for and against its use. Where I can talk about it is in relation to the law. Social media has grown and evolved at a pace much faster than the law has kept up with, and is constantly throwing up new issues that hadn't previously been contemplated by the legal system. As a result, new precedents are regularly being set, courts are having to find ways of dealing with fresh scenarios, and police, lawyers and judges are scrambling to get to grips with each new area of social media as it evolves and presents fresh challenges.

There are two main areas where time and again I find myself representing children in cases involving an online issue. One tends to centre around bullying and harassment, the other around sex and sexual relations. The common thread that runs through both is the creation of a digital footprint of which people – and particularly children – seem completely oblivious.

Malicious communications, once a little-used charge, has now become a regular term for much of the online bullying, name-calling and threats. Situations such as people using social media to vent their issues, being offensive online about someone, using insults that they wouldn't necessarily use in person – anything of that nature, put out there on a public platform, falls into the realm of malicious communications, and if reported to the police, can quickly become a legal issue.

As a defence lawyer, it is a tricky area, as in no way would I condone online bullying or harassment, but I do wonder to what degree many of the cases I deal with under this guise are really a police matter. Where do you draw the line? People have been called names and endured nasty comments for all of time, but from a legal perspective, until now most of these comments were spoken, making them therefore harder to prove, and they were rarely reported to police. Now that comment is literally there in black and white, it is a different matter. We all need to be aware of the digital footprint we are creating for ourselves, and how that can incriminate you.

We have a case at present that is effectively a falling-out between two schoolgirls who were previously close friends. One of the girls has been charged with using threatening words and behaviour, causing harassment and sending obscene communications. It centres around messages and comments she made in which she called the other girl 'fake' and threatened to beat her up; she also started a group chat on WhatsApp with other friends, in which she wrote negative comments about her.

It's not pleasant stuff, and is no doubt a horrible experience for the victim, but if the police investigated and charged every child having this kind of interaction, the courts would be full of school playground disputes … Obviously, I think this behaviour is unacceptable and needs to be tackled, but I disagree with the idea that the legal system is the way to do it. Isn't it one for the school and the parents to handle?

This is also one of so many cases that demonstrate how young people are not good at thinking about the lasting effect of what they are putting out there on social media and messaging apps about themselves and others. The defendant was focused on the initial impact of her words on her ex-friend and current friends, but gave no consideration to what it could mean for herself down the line. There is a naivety about the reach their words and actions can have, and that lack of foresight, that we looked at previously, has a definite impact. The ability to take control by doing things such as creating private groups, or determining who can follow an account, makes people feel as though they are in their own private bubble, when the reality is far from it.

Even an app such as Snapchat, which is built around the idea that what a person shares is generally only available for a short time, can have a lasting footprint. It isn't as simple as 'send a picture or message, it is seen once, then it's gone'. I'm no expert in Snapchat, but I have learned through my work how worryingly easy it is to create a fake profile – something that it is still legal to do.

I had a case where one girl was accused of assaulting another, but the victim hadn't actually seen her attacker. She assumed it was one particular girl, as they had previous history over a boy, and said that after the attack, she had been sent a laughing message from this girl on Snapchat. My trainees (who are younger and much more tech savvy than me) demonstrated within minutes how a fake profile can be created purporting to be another person, with no comeuppance or clue that the reality is otherwise. It would have been very easy for someone carrying out the assault to make it look as though someone else was responsible, with just a few minutes online.

The use of social media can also stray into organized violence, with people using it as a way to exercise their issues with others through threats, or to alert people on a wider scale as to what is about to happen. While organized fights happened long before the invention of phones or the internet – think of the clashes between rival football hooligans in the 1980s, for example – the reach is now quicker and wider, and once something is written online, that social pressure is on and people feel they have to follow through. Think of a pupil who gets into a spat with another pupil online and threatens an after-school fight – they will feel they can't back out of it once it is online for all to see. So, before you know it, we see problems played out on the street that had been initiated through bravado and whipping each other up on social media channels.

There has also been much debate around grime music and videos shared on social media platforms, and the role they can play in a court case. For example, if the video includes threats and bravado, is that something that should be used as evidence in a case, or is it a normal part of adolescent rebellion and angst or in some cases a means by which to process trauma. The law reform and human rights charity JUSTICE stated in February 2021 that the misuse of drill music to secure convictions is a profound example of the systemic racism which has left Black culture repeatedly under attack in this country. JfKL is supporting the Art Not Evidence campaign whose mission is to fight for a fairer criminal justice system by advocating for a restriction on the use of creative and artistic expression as evidence in criminal trials. Personally, I feel the use of this material in criminal proceedings perpetuates racist stereotypes and risks miscarriages of justice.

One recent example of just how much a brief social media conversation can change your life came when John Soyoye, a teenager from Manchester, was killed. Ten of his friends began a conversation on the messaging app Telegram, devastated and angry at their friend's death, and discussed possible targets for retaliation. Four of the teenagers withdrew from the conversation, and it was months later before any alleged retaliation happened, in the form of three violent assaults. But all ten were later arrested and six boys (including the four who withdrew from the chat) were convicted of conspiracy to commit grievous bodily harm and given eight-year sentences each. The other four were convicted of conspiracy to murder and sentenced to eighty-one years in total.

The case of Ademola Adedeji, one of the young men who early on withdrew from the Telegram chat, has been highlighted in the press and also in the Channel 4 documentary *Untold*, in which his friend Abayomi Oderinde explored the background to the case. Ademola's letter to the judge demonstrates perfectly how he used messaging on a group chat as a way of processing his trauma:

> I got myself into this situation due to the fact that emotions got the better of me. This was because someone I regarded as a younger brother had just been ruthlessly taken away. John was someone I shared hopes and dreams with, someone who I grew up with from the age of seven years old. I would train with him, play FIFA, and do what normal kids would do. Although he took a different path to me, I was devastated that they took his life. I was heartbroken when I found out about his death. I was on antidepressants to help me sleep. I felt as if a part of me had been taken away. This is not an excuse for the text messages I sent, I was talking out of emotion, and I absolutely did not mean a word that I said. I have apologized numerous times, and did not mean those messages I sent, and I didn't want anything to happen.

All ten of the defendants were young black men, with the prosecution building a picture around them of gangs and drill music, a stereotype the majority of them denied. Appeals are being lodged, and there are many problematic issues at play here, from racial stereotyping, to conspiracy being used in a similar way as the problematic doctrine of joint enterprise. But I mention it in this section because of social media. Telegram is considered one of the more secure, private ways to communicate, and yet those boys were still creating an incredibly damaging footprint that was to change the entire course of their lives. It really is worth thinking about what you put in writing: whether it's on Instagram or WhatsApp – everything has a permanence of sorts.

Sex and Social Media

I was initially going to keep the chapter on sex and sexuality separate to this one on social media, but I realized that, when it comes to the law, so many of the potential pitfalls and legal issues around sex and young people nowadays actually also involve social media or messaging in some way. So many of my thoughts and stories cross over between the two, that it makes sense to consider them together. I think it's fair to say that these are two areas that come to the forefront with adolescence, and navigating both of them is now a key part of coming of age, for both a child and their parents.

As the parent or responsible adult in a child's life, getting the messaging, education and timing right when it comes to sex is, of course, a very personal and ever-changing challenge. Do you take a hardline approach and leave your child potentially uneducated and keeping secrets from you? Do you take a relaxed approach, and risk giving the okay to behaviour that you really aren't okay with? There never seems to be the perfect answer. I would never comment or make judgement on the individual values that a parent chooses to instil in their child when it comes to sex, but I will share my experiences of how the law impacts on it – particularly in unexpected ways. This is especially relevant now as not only are there changing societal expectations and norms to deal with, but this whole social media thing … it's something most of us are too old to have fully experienced at that age!

The teenage years are such a tricky time, as young people are exploring who they are and discovering themselves, but social media means they can be doing this in a very public arena – and often with problematic consequences. As with other aspects of social media, the permanence, the variety of interpretation, and the wider reach than most young people seem to realize, can often be the biggest issues.

One fourteen-year-old girl I worked with had been brought up by her parents to be positive and proud of her body, and not to see it as something that needed to be hidden away or covered up. As a result, she would often post photos of herself on Snapchat and Instagram in semi-naked poses, such as in the bath with strategically placed bath bubbles; and her birthday invitation went out with a photograph of her in shorts and a bikini top that covered her nipples, but showed much of her breasts from the side. She was an attractive girl, and the pictures began to get her into some difficult situations with boys at school, who were misconstruing what she was conveying, as well as with girls, who disliked her for the attention she was garnering. So they reported her to a teacher, saying they were alarmed and distressed by the photos, and found them too provocative.

The teachers passed the concerns on to the police, and the girl was formally interviewed three times for malicious communications, which was really hard, because from her point of view, she was owning her body and her femininity. She didn't understand why she couldn't post whatever pictures of herself that she liked, and she was backed up by her parents. They were both artists, liberal minded, and extra keen to instil the idea in her that the female form is beautiful, and she should be confident to own her body and do as she liked with it.

As a lawyer brought into a case such as this, it is not for me to make a judgement on whether the pictures she was posting were appropriate or not, but fundamentally it seemed ridiculous to me that this was being treated as a criminal matter. The idea that she could have a criminal record for malicious communication because her self-expression offended some other people seemed just plain wrong.

If the school genuinely thought there was an issue, the best course of action in my mind would have been to talk to the girl and her parents about the risks, and explore ways in which she could develop that body positivity idea without potentially finding herself on the wrong side of the law. That her self-confidence could have been destroyed in any way by the actions of those involved, felt such a shame, but it is worth being aware of the way the law can view these kinds of pictures being shared by those under sixteen years of age.

If you hear someone talk about 'distributing indecent images', I imagine for most people their mind conjures up the idea of an adult taking and passing on photos of underage children, or seedy, disturbing porn. There probably isn't much of a feeling of sympathy for the person facing the charges. It is a wide-reaching term, though, and can actually be applied to teenagers – even two who are in a relationship – who send photos to each other that could be deemed pornographic. If there is any sign of a coercive element, i.e. one party saying, 'Send me a pic, please', then it might only be one of them that faces the charge, as there is an argument that the other child felt pressured into it. But if it is clearly consensual, then both can be brought in for questioning. The idea of them having 'Distributing indecent images' on their criminal record seems crazy to me. Yes, have a chat with them about what is safe, and the potential wider consequences of sharing such photos. But going to the police station for questioning seems completely disproportionate.

It became such a common issue for us that we decided to launch a whole campaign, called 'Sense About Sexting', to try and raise awareness of how children are exposing themselves to being accused of criminal offences.

I had a case in which a teenage boy had his phone checked by authorities for other reasons, but while looking they realized he had folders saved under the names of about thirty girls in his year at school. It turned out he was downloading pictures of them from Instagram and keeping them on his phone. These girls wouldn't have engaged with him in that way in person, but were happy for the extra 'like' on social media – and I think they really didn't consider the access they were giving him (and others) – but were understandably horrified to hear what he was doing.

Where do you draw the line in the access you give? I think it is such a problematic area for our young people today. And while no one should feel they need to hide their body, there needs to be more awareness of exactly who you are giving that access to. It is sometimes tough to talk about these areas without sounding like you are victim blaming, but as we unfortunately don't live in a world where everyone behaves impeccably, it is worth children tempering their behaviour in order to protect themselves. Really thinking about who has access to your posts and what you want them to take away from viewing your profile is more nuanced than just ensuring there are no paedophiles lurking.

For the boy in this example, to get this access was exciting, but he just seemed to have no idea of what was appropriate behaviour. Education on the matter needs to come from all quarters: parents, teachers, those running these social media channels, peers ... society needs to wise up to it.

As a side note, the boy also had some illegal porn on his phone that he had been sharing within a group chat with other boys at school, so he was arrested for possession of indecent images. He was completely shocked and I don't think for one minute he had considered that it was a criminal offence. In his mind it was banter with his friends, and they were just having a laugh together. So to be interviewed at the police station with his mum present was mortifying for him, and to have to explain it all to the police and his lawyer, and talk about why and what he had done, was clearly one of the worst situations of his life.

I do wonder what the long-term impact will have been on him, but equally it did need to be addressed. He took part in some sessions with the Youth Offending Team and, thankfully, the matter was eventually dealt with by way of a community resolution, thereby avoiding the stigma attached to having a criminal record for a sexual offence. It is perhaps a good reminder to all teenage boys to think about how they use social media and messaging – other people may one day see what you assumed was private, so if you know your mum would be mortified, or furious, don't do it.

The difficulty as a lawyer is often about protecting a child's position, while trying to think, 'How can this be dealt with out of court?' In one recent case, a thirteen-year-old I represented had consensual sex with a girl at a party and was arrested for engaging in sexual activity with a child. It was clearly concerning, but unless the officer gives me a clue of where he is wanting to go with it, I need to protect my client by getting him to stay quiet. As soon as he admits engaging in any sexual activity he is providing the police with the evidence to charge him with a serious sexual offence, particularly as a child aged thirteen and under is not considered in law to have the ability to consent. If there was the opportunity for a conversation about how we achieve the best outcome for both of the children involved, outside of the criminal justice system, then I would be more inclined to think it would be a safe route for my client to open up about exactly what had happened.

Interestingly, it seems very few children who are charged with a sexual offence go on to reoffend in a similar manner. Oliver Eastman, a consultant clinical psychologist for the NSPCC, who we regularly instruct in our cases, gave a talk for us recently in which he explained that only 6 to 15 per cent of those who receive support go on to reoffend in a sexual way. This shows that for most children it is very much a moment in time, an experimentation, meeting an emotional need or a lack of education that is behind it, rather than what might be considered sexual deviance.

Dr Eastman also drew our attention to a recent UK study that looked at the long-term life outcomes for young people who had shown harmful sexual behaviour as children, and were now adults. Depressingly, despite the low reoffending rate, the knock-on effect seemed apparent in other ways: nearly half (46 per cent) were rated as having unsuccessful life outcomes – unemployed, contact with mental health services, single, limited social support, unhealthy relationship with alcohol, etc.

For the 26 per cent who were deemed to have a successful life outcome – living stable and happy lives with a new positive sense of identity – the key influencing factors seemed to be educational opportunity and access to stable and supportive relationships. Where parents and extended family remained supportive and involved even after the child's initial harmful sexual behaviour, it seems to have played a key role in helping them move forward. Food for thought for anyone whose child ends up in this position, and a good reminder to look beyond a young person's offending to their broader welfare needs, rather than labelling them as sex offenders.

What about Sex and the Law Away from Social Media?

The age of consent in the UK is sixteen, regardless of your gender or the gender of the person you are having sex with. This means it is a criminal offence to have sex with anyone under the age of sixteen, no matter whether you are over or under sixteen yourself.

The other relevant legal age is thirteen. The law believes that no one under the age of thirteen is capable of giving consent to any kind of sexual contact, whether that is sex, touching or kissing. This means that, say, two twelve-year-olds choosing to engage in some kind of sexual activity, whatever the degree, are both committing a criminal offence.

So, two young people in what they consider to be a consenting relationship can clearly be committing a crime, which is something that everyone needs to be more aware of. This is not just lip service. Over the years, I have had to defend many children in this scenario, where they have been charged with sexual offences, and some who have ended up on the sex offenders register because of it.

Obviously, everyone will have a view on whether, say, sex between a fourteen- and thirteen-year-old is appropriate, and as a mother of two young boys I would certainly take issue with it. I suppose the difficulty for me is the long-term effect any arrest or charge can have on the children, who might have simply been exploring and learning about themselves. I remember that sense of wanting to fit in, and for some of the boys, in particular, it being such a genuinely painful thing that they hadn't lost their virginity when others had. So, by making it a criminal offence, it creates this sense of shame and sends the message that this is deviant behaviour, or that a sexual identity is something to be ashamed of. It worries me how that might shape a person at such a key point of their development. For a teenager to suddenly be stigmatized or labelled as a sex offender, when really they might have just been trying to work themselves out, doesn't seem right.

I would suggest that better education might bring a more satisfactory solution. As with the sharing of images discussed earlier, this issue feels more like something in which a conversation about what is appropriate and laying out some clear boundaries, might have a greater impact. Some of these children will literally only know what they are taught about sex and sexual behaviour at school, and will have had little or no guidance on the topic at home, so they can't be blamed for getting it a bit wrong along the way. Or, even if they have had talks at home, the influence of peer pressure can override all of that.

It is such a sensitive area for the police, though. While I would like them to give more consideration to the ages of the children involved, genuine consent, etc., when deciding to charge, I know that it probably feels like difficult territory for them, especially when the parents of one or both children have strong feelings on how it should be handled. Parents can have a huge influence over how cases of sex between underage teenagers are dealt with. Cases that could be sorted out by an alternative means, and where the police feel that a charge isn't necessary, can sometimes be pushed through to trial by an angry or upset parent or guardian. I have had parents who, finding out their child has had sex, refuse to believe it could be in any way consensual; that their child definitely wouldn't behave like that out of choice, and have marched them straight to the police station to report a rape.

As I am writing this, I have a client who had been in a reasonably long-term relationship with a girl. He was sixteen and she was fifteen, but they were in the same school year group. His mum worked nights and one evening he was allowed to have a few friends over. That night he and his girlfriend drank a fair bit of alcohol and took things further sexually. At one point, one of the other girls present filmed them in action, saying it was just a joke.

The girl stayed at his house the rest of the next day then, when she went home, she told her mum she had had sex. Her dad went ballistic, and contacted the boy's mother, telling her that she was a terrible parent and he was stopping his daughter from seeing her son anymore. Then, several weeks later, the video surfaced – quite a breach of trust by the friend, but unfortunately an inevitable risk, as previously discussed, around taking videos – but more crucially, the boy was arrested on suspicion of rape. Incredibly, the case has dragged on for so long, that he is now nineteen, but has only just been told that no further action is being taken. He was excluded from school as soon as the allegation was made, and has spent the last three years feeling unable to move on with this hanging over him.

So, while he and I were both extremely pleased with the outcome, it also angers me that this has had such a huge and unnecessary impact on his life. Setting aside the issues I have with the time this has taken within the legal framework, I'd really like parents to take away two things: firstly, to really think about the issue of shaming children around the topic of sex. Some young people feel shamed by it to such a degree that they feel unable to say anything other than they didn't consent, for fear of causing anger and upset. And, secondly, I'd like parents to gain an awareness of the legal implications of children engaging in sexual activity, and how potentially seriously it can be viewed in the eyes of the law.

WHERE TO GET HELP

- A UK-wide charity dedicated to preventing child sexual abuse: www.lucyfaithfull.org.uk
- The UK's leading children's charity: www.nspcc.org.uk

CHAPTER 6

Another Pandemic – County Drug Lines

I arrived at the police station to find a girl curled up in a tight ball on the chair in the interview room, her eyes darting around the room, as though looking desperately for a way out. As I tried to catch her eye with a reassuring glance, I couldn't help but notice her scrappy uneven haircut. I was told that Anna had been arrested for drug dealing charges, after being found with several bags of cannabis on her, with a street value of around £150. Looking at the fifteen-year-old in front of me, she didn't exactly look like a hardened drug dealer. It was clear that she was terrified.

As the policeman started probing her for answers as to why she had been carrying the drugs, she shrugged and stared down at her shaking hands, poking out from her dirty hoodie. It felt as if she was in no fit state to answer just yet, and I asked for a moment alone with Anna to calm her, and try and draw the story out. Little by little, it emerged that she had been tricked into visiting Cambridge from her London home by a friend, and then been held captive and forced to sell drugs by a group of older males. When she had objected, they had cut off her ponytail and forced her to perform sex acts. There was no question that she was a victim, but here she faced being charged with drug offences herself. It is a situation I see time and again in my job – this is the real face of county lines drug trafficking.

County drug lines is a phenomenon that has had a lot of coverage in the press in recent years, with stories often focused on middle-class parents in the home counties distressed at the influx of drugs to their towns and villages. It has also made appearances in TV series such as *Hollyoaks*, been the focus of BBC and Channel 4 investigations, and had an entire feature film created around it, simply called *County Lines*. It would be hard not to have heard of this growing issue. The term refers to the movement of drugs via supply chains that are set up, organized and run from cities out into the surrounding counties. It is hierarchical, organized crime, and allows people who are well versed in drug-dealing to widen the scope of their profiteering in areas that might otherwise be relatively detached from it.

Classic setups begin with what is called 'cuckooing': a drug addict in the small town is targeted and offered free drugs in return for use of their home. Before the person knows it, their home has become a drug den, and they may even find themselves completely pushed out of it, hence the term. This now becomes the local base of operation for the dealers.

The other classic and consistent feature of county lines, and the one that causes a lot of horror and indignation – exactly as it should – is the use of children to run the drugs. Children as young as twelve, carrying weapons, might be sent on public transport around the country to deliver money or drugs, or they could be selling the drugs at the instructions of someone senior, based miles away. For example, that person, armed with the main phone, might be based in Hackney in London.

They call a young person who lives in, say, Hertford and tell the child to 'Give a £20 draw of crack to so-and-so.' That child, based out of the 'cuckooed' house in Hertford, is surrounded by users, and needs to do their bidding or risk punishment.

The plain and simple reasons for the use of young people in the county lines operation is that they are considered to be less easily detected by police, they are unlikely to feel they can question orders, and they will receive lighter sentences if they are unlucky enough to be picked up and arrested. They are viewed as a malleable, disposable cog in the operation.

As well as the drug charges, the young person often risks charges for possession of weapons. They are given these weapons by their controllers for two reasons. Firstly, they are living in a home with drug addicts who can be unpredictable, so they are armed for their own protection. Secondly, they need to guard the drugs themselves, as other dealers will often rob these drug houses, knowing that mainly addicts and children are based in them, so they become like sitting targets, prey to rival gangs.

Despite the recent hype, the idea of running drug lines from cities out into the surrounding towns and villages is not a new one. I remember as a child, my own friends becoming involved in it. They would call it 'going to country', and give off an air of pride, combined with secrecy, that they were doing something important for a group of older boys who had befriended them. We were living in Bedfordshire at the time, and as well as going to small country towns, they might be sent off to Oxford for the day. When I asked one friend what he actually did there, he just shrugged, and told me: 'I just have to hold packages'.

I didn't particularly think of what was happening to them as grooming back then – I wouldn't have even really known what that was – but they were certainly drawn into it little-by-little, through preferential treatment from older, influential males. So a version of county lines was definitely around in the late nineties, but the advent of mobile phones has made it much easier.

The Mayor of London, Sadiq Khan blames the growth of county lines on cuts, lack of resources and funding. The 2017 Home Office report on the issue put it down to a combination of cuts in youth and drug recovery services, the availability of drugs, troubled family lives, poverty and school exclusions. It is clear that the dealers are one step ahead on this, and have been targeting children who fall into those categories for years. This is why I really struggle when people view the children caught up in this as criminals, focused on money or a need for respect. It is so much more complicated than that, and in reality I find most of those I represent are naive, vulnerable young people, looking for a way out of poverty or a place to belong, trying to find a way into adulthood, but often given no choice, or groomed into the behaviour before they understand what is happening and the consequences.

I have had police react in both ways – sympathetic to the arrested young person's plight, and seeing them as a victim, and then those who are adamant they were dealing drugs, and that is all that matters; they need to be charged as such. There was a push in 2019 to tackle county lines, which sounds like a great move, but I did have to wonder if it meant that these officers were going for the easy arrests of vulnerable children – picking off the low-hanging fruit – to meet targets, rather than really trying to get to the root causes.

According to the Children's Society, in 2020, the problem of county lines was responsible for an 807 per cent increase in children referred to the local authority for support in connection with modern slavery. But the services just weren't in place and ready to handle this growing need.

Sadly, I have worked on dozens of cases in this area, and see the same patterns emerging every time. The children who are targeted display an unsurprising set of characteristics, often referred to as Adverse Childhood Experiences, or ACEs. These include living in poverty, domestic violence, parental separation/divorce, a parent with a mental health condition, being the victim of abuse or neglect, having a family member in prison or growing up in a household where someone is suffering with drug or alcohol issues.

Equally, I would not like to do a disservice to many of the clients' families that I have represented who don't have those features, who have been pushed to the fringes of society through failings in the education system; or to the many children, who have had had undiagnosed Special Educational Needs, who have been demonized and portrayed as bad, excluded from school and pushed into pupil referral units, and groomed as a result of simply wanting to find a place that fits with people who accept them.

A recent client, Jack, was recruited when some older boys started to offer him free cannabis outside the school gates, or bought him chicken and chips. His stepdad had just left the family home, and it was a struggle for his mum to get the money together for basic bills each month, as well as food for him and his sister. Combine that with his own insecurities and the need to be liked, and he was flattered that these boys – men really – wanted him to hang out with them. One day he was handed a new pair of trainers and, looking down at the dirty, scuffed pair on his feet, his gratitude grew. Like most teenage boys, he was just thinking about life in the moment, and thankful for what was happening, without realizing he was creating a debt to these men. It was like drip-feeding. They were literally buying his loyalty each time the presents moved up a level. Classic grooming really, drawing children in with the lure of money and items that they are so often lacking.

Then one day Jack was asked to do a favour – just a small one, dropping off some cannabis to someone. Then, of course, the inevitable happened and the demands grew. By the time he expressed discomfort, he was too far down the line. The relationship and power dynamic had been established, and he was told: 'You know I've looked after you – now you owe me, so I need you to do me a favour.'

Before he knew it, he was fully recruited, and any inkling to say 'No' was met with fear of falling out with the people he had surrounded himself with, or the threat of violence. He felt he had no choice, and did as he was told for months, until the day he was arrested with several bags of crack cocaine, and I was called to the station to represent him.

It can be so hard for parents to step in, even when they catch wind of what is unfolding. I had one client whose father died, and while his mum tried her level best to provide a safe and loving environment for him, he was targeted due to the lack of support he was provided with in school. Disruptive behaviour then led to exclusion and, once he was taken under the wing of older peers, his mum felt powerless against them. Her car windows were smashed and a brick thrown through the windows of her house when she sought to challenge these older males.

Another mum described to me the horrible sense of losing control of her son, and trying everything she could, but still seeing him slip away. She remembers serving up Sunday dinner, her son's favourite meal of the week, and hoping they could sit and connect over it. But just as they sat down a car pulled up outside. He spotted it and told her he had to go; the fear of that person actually knocking on their front door was too much for the boy.

The young people who are drawn into county lines are predominantly male, but there are plenty of girls becoming involved too, and their numbers are growing. They are also regularly threatened with violence, although sexual grooming often comes into play as well.

The case of Abigail was referred to me after she was arrested at a drugs den in Chelmsford. Little by little she opened up to me on her situation. A friend of hers had been dating an older man. She believed he was her boyfriend, but it was clear as the story progressed that he thought otherwise, and she was one of a string of teenage girls he was seeing and grooming. He invited the two girls to Colchester for the day, but once they were hanging out at the house, Abigail quickly realized that things weren't right. Unlike her friend, she hadn't been drawn in slowly, so was shocked to suddenly have the scenario in front of her where it seemed they were being expected to stay there for the long term and sell drugs for her friend's 'boyfriend'.

Abigail objected and said she wanted to leave. The older man decided she had been rude and poured a kettle of hot water over her to 'teach her a lesson that standing up to him was not wise'. She was subsequently arrested following a police raid on the property. By the time I was involved in her case, thanks to a family friend's referral, she was in a desperate way.

In the case I mentioned at the start of the chapter, it was a friend who suggested to my client, Anna, that, as she was having a hard time at home, maybe they should get away for a couple of days to Cambridge. On the first night they stayed in a hotel, but on the second, the friend said, 'Oh, let's just stay with one of my other friends instead.' They went to a flat, and hung out with a group of older males. Anna wasn't initially aware, but they were running a drugs line from the flat. She became more uncomfortable as the evening went on, at the attention she was receiving from one of the men, and eventually she was sexually assaulted and told she couldn't leave. Determined to complete the sense of humiliation and exert their power, they cut off her pony tail and told her to sell drugs. She was held there for three weeks under constant supervision, with someone sitting in the car watching her every move as she was sent out to sell the drugs, before being arrested.

It is classic criminal exploitation – vulnerable girls are groomed, so that they feel like they are in a relationship. Before they know it, they are asked to travel out of the city to stay in a house for a few days, to deliver money. They see it as a holiday, or that they are helping their 'boyfriend', and are made to feel important for the help they are providing. But once there, they find any free will they had has disappeared. They are essentially now nothing short of modern-day slaves. It is a drip-feeding effect, and as it escalates, almost undetected, the teen is left feeling there is no way out – and often there may not be, given their powerlessness and lack of resources.

So, who is the most likely kind of child to be groomed? Often those who get drawn in are struggling emotionally with life events, have learning difficulties, or are seen as more vulnerable, and therefore are easy targets to these dealers. They might be excluded from school or be in pupil referral units – unfortunately in my experience these educational units are a fertile ground for this kind of situation. Other children might be living in care. Those who lack a guiding figure, or have little adult influence in their life, who have more spare time to be hanging around with others and fewer people worrying about what they are up to, are typical targets.

I had one young client who was placed in a particular children's home in west London and, within a day, he and two girls were taken to a crack house in Surrey. They were found there soon after with large quantities of drugs and in possession of weapons. Possibly someone at the children's home was even involved in facilitating the exploitation, and certainly there were huge red flags around the running of this home. This might have been a record time for a child to be taken from a home, but I have sadly seen this happen far too frequently.

The idea that any of these children are viewed as criminals as opposed to victims is upsetting. Do you think they want to be in a situation like that out of choice? I have endless examples from throughout my career – even as I write this I am working through a harrowing county lines case. Every case is heartbreaking in its own way, and the fact that this cycle is being allowed to continue, with the young people taking the brunt of it all, given what we know about it and the signals that enable us to recognize it, really angers me.

One young girl who was arrested was sitting crying in interview when I arrived, and was telling the officer that she had drugs in her vagina that she had been forced to carry. It was a horrific case, and the officer could clearly see it for what it was, and referred to her as a victim in his report. But still the CPS took the decision to charge. Talking to this girl the day they pushed ahead with that, and effectively telling her her life was now on hold until the courts had time to process her, was so hard. She was terrified of what those who effectively controlled her would do, and as so many children do, no longer felt able to give evidence in her defence for fear of reprisals. It was only when we gathered a great deal of compelling evidence together that the CPS dropped the case – eight months down the line and a week before trial.

That wasn't even a long delay compared to some cases. Sometimes these young people can be in the court process waiting to be seen for over two years. The waiting game can have all sorts of impacts on them, for example, a loss of friends and a sense of isolation, disruption to their education or career choices, depression or other mental health issues, a loss of trust, being stigmatized by others … the list is endless.

For many of the children drawn into county drug lines, section 45 of the Modern Slavery Act provides a defence. Effectively, if you are under eighteen and accept that you have been in possession of drugs, or selling drugs, but can prove it was as a direct consequence of modern slavery, then you have the protection of the law and should not be prosecuted.

For those over eighteen, it is necessary to prove not only that they were compelled to commit the offence as a direct consequence of modern slavery, but also that a reasonable person in the same situation as them and having the same characteristics (age, sex, and physical or mental illness or disability) would have no realistic alternative to committing that offence. This is much more difficult to prove and something that juries struggle to comprehend.

The National Referral Mechanism

In order for a person to be recognized by the state as a victim of trafficking or modern slavery they have to be referred through an assessment process called the National Referral Mechanism (NRM). However, despite the solicitor often being the first person a victim can disclose the extent of their experiences to, they are unable to refer their clients through the NRM process. Instead, people such as police officers, social workers, some Youth Offending Team officers, or specially trained teams from the Salvation Army have the authority to be what is called a 'first responder', which gives them the ability to refer a child found in what appears to be a county line situation through the NRM. This used to hold a lot of weight in court, so that if a positive, conclusive, grounds decision was made on that young person by the NRM, then the CPS would frequently decide not to prosecute.

The problems started because no one had envisaged just how vast the numbers of children being exploited and groomed into committing criminal offences could be, so the use of that defence reached epidemic proportions. As people became more knowledgeable and aware of this route, it gained traction, and the NRM process became completely overwhelmed. They didn't have enough staff to deal with the demand, so it could take a year for someone to get a decision on whether they were a victim of trafficking or modern-day slavery or not. Where it was often pertinent to the young person's defence, the trial couldn't go ahead without that information, so the court would keep adjourning, and the criminal justice system was becoming swamped. Additionally, if a child has been deemed to be the victim of exploitation, social services are supposed to safeguard that child, but the huge rise in situations being flagged meant they didn't have the resources to do that either. The service is in a complete mess, with a huge backlog.

The Home Office has published its statistical bulletin providing a summary and breakdown of the number of potential victims of modern slavery referred to the NRM in 2022. In that year, the NRM received a total of 16,938 referrals, which represents an increase of 33 per cent from the previous year. Of all the referrals received, at least 7,019 (41 per cent) related to children. This is the highest number of referrals received since the NRM began in 2009.

The Home Office bulletin breaks down the referrals by gender, exploitation type and nationality. It confirms that:

- 80 per cent of potential child victims referred to the NRM were male (5,607) and 20 per cent were female (1,978)

- The most common form of exploitation reported for potential child victims was criminal exploitation

- 2,281 referrals were specifically flagged for county lines. Seventy-five per cent of those referrals related to male children

- UK nationals represented the second highest nationality referred to the NRM. Of all of the UK nationals referred to the NRM, 80 per cent were potential child victims

However, rather than recognizing modern slavery among young people caught up in county drug lines as the epidemic it is, the court of appeal decided to try and narrow the possibility of this defence being used. In a case called *R v Brecani*, it was decided that being deemed a victim by the NRM was not enough, and was no longer admissible in court. How nonsensical that a government body set up to carry out the assessments was now effectively being determined as not qualified to do so. For anyone wanting to run that defence, the onus was now on us as lawyers and solicitors to prove our clients were the victims of exploitation, by calling an expert in county lines, and providing significant supplementary evidence. This is all well and good if the young person has been known to social services or similar for a long time, but if they have stayed below the radar until now, where does the evidence come from?

I had one boy who was groomed over the course of three years, and in that time period there were school records that showed a long history of concerns around him, statements from his mum when he began to go missing, social service records of concern, psychology reports ... Add those to a report from Dr Grace Robinson, a leading expert in the field, and we had a good defence case. Strong enough that the CPS dropped the case, but only a week before trial, so they really kept us hanging until the last minute. (Dr Robinson completed her PhD 'Urban Street Gangs, Child Criminal Exploitation and County Lines' in 2019 and founded Black Box Research, an organization whose primary aim is to support victims and increase awareness of modern slavery.)

I have other clients, though, for whom there isn't that long history of documentation, where they weren't known to social services until their arrest for this offence, and where that lack of a paper trail makes theirs a difficult case to defend, despite the fact they are no less a victim of slavery than the other boy.

Clearly, the hope with the *Brecani* ruling was that people wouldn't turn to this defence, as it is so difficult to supply what is needed. But for me that is not tackling the real issue at stake but hiding it, simply to get cases through court that bit quicker.

I am finding more and more children are being prosecuted as, following the change in law, there have been further cases limiting the weight of expert evidence. Sadly, in order to have any chance of winning their cases, I am having to prepare clients to give evidence. It seems that the only way to persuade a judge or jury that these young people have been a victim is through their own words, but I really struggle as to how we got here. These children have experienced significant trauma and some have been diagnosed with PTSD, yet the criminal justice system risks exacerbating their symptoms and re-traumatizing them by forcing them to tell their stories while giving evidence in court.

What happens to a child who has been through the criminal justice system, been charged, and is out on bail while waiting for their court hearing – or has even been found to be a victim of slavery, exonerated, and is sent back to 'normal' life?

Unfortunately, this is a big problem. Those people who got them into county lines in the first place have not disappeared, nor has the hold that they have over that young person. If anything, it has increased as, inevitably, any drugs that were on them at the time of their arrest have been confiscated. So actually their debt to their handler has grown, and they are under further pressure to do more work for the gang to recoup the losses.

I had one lad who was picked up in Buckinghamshire, clearly sent there as part of a county drug-trafficking line. Within weeks of his arrest, he was found in Carlisle with drugs, having been threatened that he needed to earn back the £600 that he had 'lost' when the drugs were confiscated during his first arrest. His debt increased, he became more desperate, and he was again arrested, this time in Cambridge. The spiral was worsening, and he was getting deeper into trouble with each arrest. I've had so many cases where you can follow the chronology of this horrible web that these children are becoming further entangled in.

Social services often don't know what to do, as they are presented with a child who is being controlled and used by someone who exerts much more power over them than the social worker can. Add to this that the child doesn't always immediately identify themselves as a victim – they might think that they are doing a job and this is normal, or simply be too scared to just say, 'Yes, I am being made to do this, or I will be hurt.' It can take a great deal of time and skill to put together a decent package of support for the young person, even after it has been determined by the court that there are conclusive grounds to believe they are a victim of exploitation. In the meantime, very little changes in the young person's life, and the cycle continues.

Additionally, of course, with each arrest there is less sympathy – although as part of the defence we will be very vocal in pointing out that there have been no further interventions from social services since the young person was last up in court. Thankfully we have had some judges who can see this for what it is, and say, 'Well, the CPS need to take a view then, because if there is a chance they are still being exploited, and nothing is being done to change that, do we really have a case here?'

Until you actually put the funding into properly supporting these children, nothing is going to change. But that is a much more significant undertaking. It would take so many more resources in social care, extra training for police, and the engagement of community groups. These need to contain trusted individuals creating safe spaces for children to disclose what is happening and receive support that is tailor-made for them.

There is a developing area of best practice founded by Professor Carlene Firmin, an applied social researcher at Durham University, who founded the concept of contextual safeguarding. Professor Firmin's research has established a framework which responds to young people's experiences of harm outside the home and challenges traditional child protection approaches by harnessing communities, which is essential in disrupting exploitation and keeping children safe. Social services swooping in and moving a child to Wales, for example, away from any support networks they do have, is not the answer. But most public services have a limited remit, finite resources and an inability to innovate and really engage with young people and their families in a way that works for them. Until this is fixed, the children – the low-hanging fruit again – will continue to take the brunt of arrests, leaving those controlling them and profiting from them at fairly low risk of prosecution.

The other reason to really put the resources into getting these groomed kids fully out of the situation, is that, sadly, down the line, they might climb the ladder and be asked to recruit younger children themselves, therefore perpetuating the cycle. I've had clients who in their twenties have climbed the ranks in a drug-dealing network, and are now actively recruiting children to act as runners. If they had been helped when they were at that early stage, things might have been different, but now they have become part of the problem.

Initially, Lucy was groomed sexually by a county line gang, from a very young age. Social services were aware of it, and moved her into a secure children's home, but this didn't prevent the gang from gaining access to her. Her sexual favours became her entire identity, the one powerful thing she effectively felt she had. Over time, this sexual exploitation became criminal exploitation, as she became a more trusted individual in the group. Lucy began dealing too, brought in other girls to work for the network, and brought drugs into prison. By the time of her arrest, a snapshot of her life then showed her as a willing and key part of the group, so any defence of grooming or coercion was deeply hidden. The officer in the case described her offending as 'a lifestyle choice'. But had the very clear grooming process been fully addressed when Lucy was being sexually exploited at twelve years old, the outcome could have been very different.

It is really sad looking back over the number of cases I have dealt with to do with county drug lines. Reading back through them when researching for this book, there were even more than I initially remembered, and so few of them with real, solid solutions that have taken the young person out of the situation and given them the tangible help they need. I think most people don't know what is going on, as it is happening just beneath the surface of society, but you don't have to look far to find it. For parents, it is really important to understand what some of these children are experiencing and to be able to spot any signs in their own child before it is too late. For children, I want them to understand the consequences of what they are getting caught up in, but also that there is help out there.

Signs to Watch Out For

- a child going missing from school or home and/or being found out of their area
- unexplained acquisition of money, clothes or mobile phones
- excessive receipt of texts/phone calls, and/or having multiple handsets
- relationships with controlling/older individuals or groups
- leaving home/care without explanation
- unexplained injuries
- carrying weapons
- self-harm or significant changes in emotional well-being
- sexual violence – this is a tool of exploitation used particularly but not exclusively against girls
- getting into trouble with the police for low-level offending such as theft

WHERE TO GET HELP

It is so important as a parent to remember that it is not your fault if your child does get drawn into county drug lines, and that there is help out there. Some websites I would suggest exploring are:

- **Abianda:** a social enterprise that works with young women and girls affected by gangs and county lines. Also provides training for the professionals who work with them. www.abianda.com

- **Children's Society:** runs various programmes aimed at preventing, educating, and disrupting county drug lines, as well as helping rehabilitate anyone who has experienced it. www.childrenssociety.org.uk/what-we-do/our-work/child-criminal-exploitation-and-county-lines

- **St Giles Trust:** working in various locations across the UK to help people whose lives have taken a downturn, they provide support to vulnerable young people who have been exploited, education within the wider community, and are also working towards prevention. www.stgilestrust.org.uk

- **Power the Fight:** a charity tackling violence affecting young people by looking to long-term solutions and acting as a link between the community and policy makers. www.powerthefight.org.uk

- **Safer London:** works with young people in the capital who are affected by exploitation, or are at risk of being exploited, with the focus on making them feel safe. www.saferlondon.org.uk

CHAPTER 7

When Children's Homes Go Wrong

Think about the worst argument you have ever had with your child, and how they reacted. Maybe they kicked the kitchen door, damaging it, maybe they pushed you in frustration, or lashed out at their brother, or maybe they stormed out of the house and 'ran away' to a friend's home, announcing they hated you and were never coming back. Would you call the police and risk seeing them prosecuted for criminal damage or assault? Or would you shout at them/ground them/explain why that was unacceptable once things had calmed down?

I'm going to take a guess that it would be one of the latter options, which would be a natural parental response. Unfortunately this is not the case in care homes, where the police are regularly called out for incidents such as those mentioned above, which goes some way to explaining why children in care are *six* times more likely to be criminalized than other children.

A children's home provides care and accommodation for young people who, for whatever reason, cannot live with a parent. It is often because of a breakdown in the family unit due to death, illness, disability, neglect or abuse, or because the child has complex needs that a parent feels unable to cope with. The purpose of the home is to provide housing and care for that young person for the short, medium or long term, as dictated by circumstances.

While in the homes, the children are considered to be 'looked after' by the local authority, so the local authority becomes their corporate parent when it comes to making decisions about their situation. In the home, the staff are more directly carrying out this role, although in my experience many of them take a heavy-handed approach, and the decision to involve the police when an issue arises is made far too readily.

The first point of contact we have with any child being prosecuted following an incident in a children's home tends to be when we are called to the police station. Inevitably the purported offence will be assault or criminal damage. More often than not, the first thing we will do is try to take everything back a step by reminding everyone that the local authority is a corporate parent, and if this incident had happened in a family home between, say, a child and a parent or a sibling, would they be looking to prosecute? We'll encourage those involved to look at the policy of the home and consider whether this situation really is something that steps outside of the boundaries of acceptable behaviour, and whether it has been correctly dealt with.

One situation in which it was clear that it hadn't been correctly dealt with, arose when we represented a boy called Liam, who had never been in trouble with the police before. He had been in a care home for a while, and became close to a boy called Aidan, a couple of years younger than him. When Liam, who was fifteen at the time, was moved on to a new home, they kept in touch. One night Aidan went missing from his care home. He was upset, and turned up to see Liam, who took him in, as any friend would. When the police were called about the missing boy, they came to see if he was hiding out with Liam, but Liam refused to let them into his bedroom.

At this point there should have been conversations about why the boys were upset, explanations as to why Aidan had felt the need to seek out his friend for support, and discussions with care home staff involved with the boys' welfare. But for whatever reason, that didn't happen, and these police officers decided that dealing with it physically was the way forward. Things rapidly escalated. The officers forced entry and tasered both boys on the basis that they had resisted arrest, and Liam was consequently charged with assaulting an emergency worker.

As a side note on this aspect, I don't think any emergency workers should be subjected to any kind of assault when carrying out their job. But the term 'assault' does instantly conjure up the worst kind of behaviour, and that often isn't the case. Anything that leaves any kind of mark on the worker is recorded as assault, to the point where I've even had a court case where the 'assault' was a graze on an officer's finger, obtained during the arrest. So in certain cases I say 'assault' with some degree of reservation.

These officers were meant to be going there to encourage Aiden to go back to his home, but instead this heavy-handed behaviour meant that both these kids ended up arrested. Now, put that same situation into play but for children who still live at home with families. A child goes missing. The assumption is he will have headed to his friend Liam's house. One set of parents might call the other: 'Is my kid at yours? Could you send him home?'

Liam's mum might talk to Aidan to find out what was going on, what he is struggling with, and encourage him to go home: 'What's happening? Your mum really wants to speak to you, and you can't just stay here.'

It is highly unlikely that the situation is going to escalate to the point of police officers being called, bursting in, and physically restraining them, or even the parents deciding to take a physical approach themselves.

So, apply the situation to a normal family home, and it suddenly looks very different. It is normal behaviour for kids to run away to a mate's; the important thing is how you approach that situation. If I'd been working in the care home, I'd have been encouraging Liam to open the door and chat to me or the police, and addressed with Aidan what his concerns were. But I would also be telling the police that while we were happy to support them in what is their duty of care to return Aidan to his home, 'You're not going to approach our young people in that way. Liam is a child, he is bonded with his friend over their shared trauma and care experience, and is looking out for him, so let's bring it down a level, please.'

There are ways to manage the situation that don't see a boy who was looking out for his friend, and was not being supported by the people who are meant to be acting as his surrogate parents, ending up in the criminal justice system.

Thankfully, there is a growing understanding within the CPS that many incidents occurring in children's homes should not be prosecuted when the issue is something such as damaging a door, or arguing with a fellow resident. Low-level incidents that are just part of growing up should be handled internally in the home, as they would be in a family situation. This is why the CPS have now put a ten-point checklist in place to work through when deciding whether to prosecute someone from a children's home. The points are:

- What is in the behaviour policy of the children's home?
- Why have the police been involved and is it as agreed in the policy?

- Has any informal/disciplinary action already been taken?
- Has there been an apology or reparation?
- What are the victim's views?
- What are the social worker's views?
- What is the care plan for the looked-after child?
- What is said of the recent behaviour of the looked-after child?
- What information has the looked-after child shared about the incident?
- Are there any aggravating or mitigating features?

There are still times, though, when I raise these points at the police station and officers look at me blankly, or the professionals in court don't seem to realize that this checklist exists. There are still too many arrests happening, and prosecutions getting through the cracks, that only get dropped when we make representations to the CPS. The resources being put into these cases, whether to the CPS, or in legal aid to us, are such a waste of time, and ones that could be avoided with a little more use made of that list.

Why are Children's Homes Failing?

People who have never come into contact with a children's home tend to have one of two extreme images of them. Either something akin to the cruel orphanages of Victorian Britain, with long, cold dormitories filled with metal bedframes, and children forced to scrub floors each day. Or they think of the idyllic, warm and nurturing image, where everyone lives a happy, problem-free life with an almost surrogate family, conjured up in more recent televised portrayals, such as *The Story of Tracy Beaker*. It would be fair to say, neither are true reflections of the reality. Children's homes tend to be converted residential properties with up to six children living there at a time, under the supervision of key workers, with bedrooms, bathrooms, and communal areas. But that is about as far as the similarities go.

There were 2,462 children's homes in the UK as of 2021, an 11 per cent increase on the year before, and the quality can vary greatly, mostly, I believe, because 75 per cent of them are now privately run. Originally, all children's homes were run by the local authority, but over the last twenty years many of these have been closed down, often for financial reasons, with the work then being outsourced. This means that while people will have all sorts of motivation for running the home, they are all effectively businesses, so profit is going to be a driving force.

You would assume that to open a children's home, the list of requirements such as qualifications and background checks would be high. You are, after all, about to be in charge of a group of young people, the majority of whom have already gone through a degree of trauma, or at the very least, challenges, in their lives. But the reality is that with a bit of capital and some basic form-filling, shockingly, most people are able to open a home. People make a house suitable for multiple occupancy, hire staff and get them checked by the Disclosure and Barring Service (DBS). This flags criminal convictions, and DBS checks are needed for certain jobs and volunteer roles where someone might be looking to work with children, the elderly or vulnerable people. The would-be children's home owner is now able to offer their services to the local authority, who, with their own homes closed, have a shortage, and often appear as though they are not fussy at all about the home's credentials.

In terms of the staff, again you get a whole range, but a person can be hired without any qualifications, as long as they start working towards a relevant qualification once in the role. There are guidelines that say there should be at least a four-year age gap between the staff member and the oldest child in the home, but this means some of the staff aren't much older than the children themselves. While they can perhaps provide a friendly ear, it doesn't really allow them to take on a nurturing, stable, guiding, surrogate-parent type of role, which is often the person that these children really need. It also means they are rarely sufficiently trained to de-escalate situations – once again contributing to the increase in events that then become police matters.

Of course, it doesn't mean that all homes are sub-standard, but it means there is very little consistency across the board, and plenty of them drop below what, to me, is an acceptable standard. I had one client at a privately run home in Luton, and as soon as I walked in the door, I was impressed. Everything from the way the staff called him to the meeting, to the great food I could smell coming from the kitchen, meant that it felt like a warm and nurturing environment, where the people working there clearly had the best interests of the children at heart. They had created a real home.

Then this young person was moved to another home in Wembley, and when I visited him there, the house was messy. The few staff on duty were cold in their attitude, and there was nowhere private in the house that we could sit and chat. It is a bit like visiting elderly care homes: you can visit a children's home and be blown away by the ethos and values, and feel like the staff really care and the person running it has all the best motivations; then you go to another in which it seems merely to be about meeting the bare minimum basic needs, the staff have very little interest in those there as individuals, and the home is just existing to make a profit.

The way a child initially goes into a home, is that their situation might have been flagged up by social services, the police, or by parents themselves, and then they will either be removed through a care order, or the parents are asked to voluntarily agree to social services accommodating their child under section 20 of The Children's Act. Foster homes – in which the child is placed in a family environment with one or two foster parents – are also an option, but there is a shortage of these across the country compared with the number of children in need of one, and sometimes it is decided that a children's home is better for their situation anyway.

Parents might imagine wraparound help for their child, and some think that a fresh environment might do them good. The child might also be keen to go, thinking they are going to be living independently or escaping the troubles of home. But the reality is, it rarely fulfils the hopes of either party. Whether consciously, or subconsciously, the message that most children take from being put into care is that nobody cares about them, and they are much more likely to be exploited once there, or get in trouble with the law.

I've had cases of children running away, fighting, getting involved in county lines, being groomed … all literally within days of going into a care home. They are emotionally vulnerable and easy targets, more so than many other children, so to think they aren't getting the protection they deserve is heartbreaking.

I would like to see a lot more scrutiny into children's homes: they need to be about so much more than just providing a bed. What are we really trying to achieve from them? These homes are paid a lot of money, and what the children are getting in return is often not good enough.

I hate visiting homes that have no communal areas for children to chill out and interact in, or that might encourage them to eat a meal with a key worker. That is a clear sign to me that profit has taken priority – the owners would rather have one more bedroom to house an extra child and have maximum occupancy, than a shared room that could improve the inhabitants' lives. There needs to be a higher focus on keeping the homes' values based on nurturing the individual child.

The other issue I have seen is that some homeowners are incredibly militant about the young person's finances. Once they are sixteen and are perhaps starting to work towards leaving care, a child is given a certain amount of money each week by their social worker, with the idea that they will begin to learn about budgeting. I visited one home that was taking the attitude that if the children contributed some of that money towards each meal, they could eat, otherwise they had to do without. I understand trying to teach children the value of money, but it is a learning curve, and to have children sitting and watching while others eat their dinner, not able to join in the meal, seems utterly Dickensian. What message are you giving that child? A parent wouldn't treat them like that, so why would the home?

Recruitment and training needs to be improved in so many of these homes, and I'd like to see call-outs to police monitored and impacting negatively on rights to tender, as it suggests that staff aren't suitably qualified or equipped to work with children if they can't support them without police intervention.

I am sure a lot of local authorities are aware they are substandard really, but they are so reliant on these private homes now, as they have effectively handed over all the power. In my mind, they should scrap the whole lot, set a higher basic standard and make the homes tender for contracts from scratch with proof that children and not profit really are at the heart of all their plans.

WHERE TO GET HELP:

- **Family Action:** If you are a young person leaving care, this service offers practical and emotional support www.family-action.org.uk
- **Become:** A charity supporting young people in care and young care leavers to unleash their potential www.becomecharity.org.uk/about-become
- **Coram Voice:** A leading children' rights organization www.coramvoice.org.uk

CHAPTER 8

Neurodiversity, Mental Health and the Law

Life for a young person with neurodiversity or a mental health condition tends to throw up more challenges than for most, whether that is getting up in the morning, interpreting social cues, or making sense of the words in a schoolbook. So imagine if I told you that these children are also much more likely to get caught up in the criminal justice system. Quite shocking, isn't it? And in many ways it seems unfair. Life is already a tricky journey to navigate for these young people – and their parents too – so how does it end up that they are more likely to catch the attention of the police? For such a pressing issue, the link between the two has not been explored nearly as much as it should have been. I am talking about everything from autism and ADHD, to speech or cognitive problems, post-traumatic stress disorder (PTSD), and at the sharpest end, psychosis. Traits or pitfalls that come hand-in-hand with their struggles can all cause a young person to become caught up with the law.

Mental health issues among young people have significantly risen after the Covid-19 pandemic, but the services are not there to deal with it. Waiting lists for Child and Adolescent Mental Health Services (CAMHS) are over twelve months long; it feels like a ticking time bomb.

Why Are They More Likely to End Up in Court?

There are many reasons why a young person dealing with mental health struggles might end up in court, but it often comes down to a failure to diagnose in the first place, which has then meant that when that young person is in crisis, those around them don't know how to deal with it, so rather than de-escalating the situation, they end up escalating it. Without a diagnosis, there is a complete lack of understanding as to why their behaviour is taking place. Even if it has been diagnosed, the problem that ends up in court can be down to a failure to engage with that young person in a way that aligns with the diagnosis, and is therefore conducive to getting a good outcome.

Autism

Of the various mental health conditions that crop up among children we work with at JfKL, autism is the one that is the most frequently undiagnosed. It is highly frustrating that so many children have their daily lives impacted by the condition from a young age, only for it to be missed entirely and left undiagnosed until secondary school. Sometimes you see an offence specifically aligning with autistic traits – think of certain high-profile cases, such as that of Gary McKinnon, who hacked into the Pentagon, and where experts picked up on his autism through signs such as his narrow attention span, obsession with technology, and lack of awareness of how others might perceive his actions – but it can present itself in many ways. Misunderstood social cues leading to altercations; a difficulty in making friends leading to social exclusion; vulnerabilities and a lack of awareness of risk that then leads on to exploitation – there are a whole host of ways autism can contribute to a young person's journey to becoming caught up in the legal system.

Imagine an autistic teenager sitting on a train. Their natural eye contact and body language can often be unintentionally different to the societal norm. Another boy on the train takes offence at a refusal to make eye contact, makes a comment, and the typical reaction of a person with autism would be to give a frank or blunt reply. The other boy thinks he is being mocked and insults get thrown, with tensions quickly escalating. The confused autistic teen lashes out in a panic, and is arrested for assault. There is no question that it is assault. We have mitigating circumstances, but that won't change his subsequent record.

I had one teenage client who really struggled to process the end of romantic relationships, and genuinely couldn't understand how to move forward. He would incessantly call and message the ex-partner, leading to him being prosecuted for harassment on at least three occasions.

Often, the autistic traits might be below the surface for much of a person's life, as they have learned to mask the signs so well, but then a triggering moment will draw out a strong reaction, and that might be all it takes for the law to get involved. It is unacceptable that these scenarios could have been allowed to develop in the first place.

Other Common Conditions

I see a fair number of children with ADHD passing through the doors of JfKL, mainly because the impulsive trait that exists in most young people is even higher in those with ADHD. As a result, it can lead to behavioural issues and difficulties in emotional regulation. These children often end up in trouble for fights, and have a high risk of exclusion from school for issues such as shouting out comments in class, or not thinking before they speak to a teacher, meaning they are considered consistently difficult.

Speech and language developmental delay is another common neurological trait we see in our clients, but young people are incredibly resilient and creative at finding ways around it and disguising their struggles. One young person I worked with was diagnosed with quite a severe developmental delay, but he had taught himself a key set of catchphrases and 'street' language that he would use for every response. His peers didn't notice, as he had become so used to masking what was actually a significant language issue.

We also see children who are on medication for conditions such as anxiety and depression, who are struggling to cope with day-to-day life. Some of them are showing traits of bipolar disorder, and while psychiatrists are reluctant to diagnose that at a young age, it seems from my experience that when mental health issues such as these are left untreated, entry into the legal system becomes a higher probability.

Undiagnosed Mental Health Issues

How a person's mental health presents when it comes to the attention of the law can be divided into two main strands:

- People with significant mental health issues, who fall into crime as a result of them
- Those with undiagnosed mental health issues, which are only discovered as a result of a crime

This second category is unfortunately huge. I have a great deal of personal experience in terms of recognizing mental health issues and educational needs in a young person, but as a matter of course we tend to have psychological assessments on most clients anyway, to be sure to pick up on anything. It is actually quite straightforward to get a report authorized – the funding from the Legal Aid Agency can be authorized within a couple of days – the more frustrating aspect is the waiting list of six to eight weeks for a psychiatrist or psychologist.

Sometimes the full extent of a child's vulnerability doesn't become apparent until they've gone through a full psychological assessment, which might not be available until months into your case.

There are so many children who have gone through primary education with the school taking a nurturing approach and managing their emotional needs on an individual level. So a teacher might adapt to different needs and perhaps recognize that a young person works better if they are told what the plan for the day is, or that they need to sit next to certain other children, or be placed in a small group. We also find that if another child in the class has a clear SEND, and has been assigned a teaching assistant, our clients who *haven't* been diagnosed are sat next to them, and the teaching assistant ends up also working with them too. At other times they are placed next to a more able child, who ends up helping them. Basically, the teachers are often adept at adjusting.

But primary school teachers might have never added up the multiple different adjustments made for and by a child, as perhaps between teacher and child they have managed them so well that in the end they hardly notice them. Or perhaps the adjustments don't appear acute enough that the teacher feels they reach the threshold to refer the child for an educational healthcare plan.

Then that child goes into secondary school and suddenly – bang! – they can't cope. It is such a massive shock to the system that they react in all sorts of ways that aren't appropriate to the environment, but they can't express what is going wrong. Instead, they simply come across as belligerent and difficult. In a school of what might be a thousand pupils it is hard for a teacher to pick up on, so soon the child is just labelled for behaving badly. Unless there is a professional who can see that this might be a reaction to an underlying condition, then their behaviour will be managed, perhaps until the point they are excluded. Then there will be no one to intervene at all.

Then you have parents who are taking a similar approach at home, who are used to the way their child operates and what gets the best out of them, and they won't even recognize that they have adapted their whole way of life to suit the child's special needs. Because that is what they have always done, they don't know that the approaches they are taking are very different to someone whose child doesn't have any kind of neurodiversity.

I might meet a child for the first time at the police station, or at a first hearing, and it will become apparent to me quite quickly that there is an underlying condition. Then, speaking to a parent, there will be aspects that flag up, such as the child's insistence on eating only one kind or colour of food, a reference to a struggle learning to read, or a need for a strict routine, a series of steps they have to take just to ensure their child gets to school on time, or an acknowledgment of endless trouble with the school. I'll suggest we have an expert check them for a diagnosis, and almost inevitably my suspicions will be confirmed. It is so sad that the first time this child is diagnosed with autism or ADHD, or language issues, is when they enter the criminal process.

How do the Police and Courts React?

As with so many areas, it feels as if the law has not kept abreast with developments in neurodiversity and mental health.

In my experience there is a lack of police training when it comes to dealing with children with mental health issues. From the outset, the whole police approach is to do things in a set way, with very little room for manoeuvre, in a manner that I generally feel is quite confrontational. Even when an officer might realize they are dealing with someone who is neurodiverse or with mental health issues, it seems as if they can often take on a stance of fear or anger, which isn't helpful, and can heighten the problem. As autism becomes more widely understood I believe there is more training available to the police, but it is down to each force as to how much of a priority this is. Institutions such as the National Autistic Society have inexpensive online training specifically aimed at the police – surely that should be used more widely?

We had a client who was playing with a traffic cone and a policeman approached him in quite a confrontational way, things escalated, and we are now representing him for assault on an emergency worker. Of course, initially the officer wasn't to know that the teen was autistic, but the Body Worn camera footage clearly shows that he wasn't approached in a way that was at all conducive to resolving the situation and, autistic or not, it would have been intimidating for him. But when a child gives off clear signs of his condition, as this boy did – in fact he actually told the officer he was autistic and presented a card he carried that stated this – I think officers with enough training would realize that adjusting their approach would be appropriate.

Because difficulties reading body language, social cues and communication issues are so common in those with neurodiversity, navigating a situation such as being confronted by a police officer can feel well beyond their capabilities. Their confused or defensive response can be seen as obstructive by officers, and the situation often escalates. But a trained officer who recognized the signs could potentially bring the tension down a level and draw things to a more successful conclusion.

I had one young boy who was autistic, attended a special education school, and had a fight in the playground with a girl who was also autistic. At the station, the officer obviously thought he would need to try a different approach for this interview, and I appreciate that aspect – that he was aware the usual interview technique might not work – but he opted for the Truth and Lies Discussion (TLD) test: the one used to see if child witnesses understand the difference.

The TLD has to be carried out on tape as part of the recorded interview. The officer will give a simple example and ask the child to confirm whether it is a truth or lie, so for example: 'If we look at my pen, my pen is red. But what if I told you that pen was blue, what would you say? Is that the truth or a lie?'

But, you cannot use that test on children being treated as suspects, as they have the right not to incriminate themselves, and talking about truth and lies could potentially mean they do exactly that.

So often the questioning of children with special educational needs – social communication issues and autism in particular – is awful. The sentences will be too long, the legal language will be too complicated and worst of all is the use of theoretical questions. Asking someone with autism about an intangible, theoretical scenario, a 'what if' type of question, is very difficult for them to respond to. It means I have to sit in these interviews interrupting practically every question in order to make it something my client can understand. There needs to be a serious improvement in the training on offer to police in this area.

When it comes to court, I've found it to be a real mixed bag with judges and magistrates. Some are clearly very au fait with the issues that come with neurodiversity and mental health conditions and reflect this within their approach to the children in court, while others seem a little less keen to engage. There are, however, updated sentencing guidelines, released in 2020, that they are supposed to consider, called 'Sentencing offenders with mental disorders, developmental disorders, or neurological impairments'. Plus, judges and magistrates are naturally very evidence-focused, so are keen to see our psychological or psychiatric assessment, which is generally a good starting point.

I'm not saying that someone with mental health struggles should be instantly excused, but the court experience needs to be adjusted to their needs to make it a fairer process, and due consideration does need to be given to their situation when it comes to sentencing. For example, a child with special educational needs is more vulnerable to grooming into a negative peer group, as they often feel like outsiders in society and just want to be accepted. And with even less foresight than most children, are they really likely to have played a significant part in a drug deal, or simply been following the instructions of someone else?

The teenager with autism I mentioned earlier, who struggled with the end of relationships, went about the rest of his life without too much difficulty and was not involved in any other crime. The sensible outcome to me would have been a package of support to undertake specific counselling that assisted him in navigating these particular circumstances with which he struggled. Counselling would have improved both his life and that of any future partners, without the distress of court, where he would have been incapable of giving evidence in his own defence.

We once had a client who came through the Youth Justice Legal Centre (a project we set up to focus on training and practising reform among the youth criminal justice profession), because she was being prosecuted for offences against the highway. It turned out that her crime was attempting to take her own life by jumping from a road bridge. The justification was that she might cause an accident in the process, but she was mentally unwell and suicidal and obviously needed counselling and support to get her on a better path – something that a criminal conviction clearly wasn't going to do.

I represented Sophie in court in a county town outside London. She was facing a charge of affray and assaulting a police officer, after an incident at a train station. The hearing didn't get off to a good start when I said I was from JfKL – the magistrates visibly baulked at the idea of a 'leftie London lawyer working for a charity', daring to come down and work on one of their cases, as generally it was the same few lawyers who worked across all the cases there.

Sophie had admitted to everything in an interview at the police station, but had apparently struggled to show any remorse for it. The courts were under the assumption that she would be pleading guilty at the hearing when I had become her lawyer, but without showing remorse, she wasn't eligible for a caution.

However, her parents told me that Sophie had just been diagnosed with autism and pathological demand avoidance (PDA), which means that a person will go to extreme lengths to avoid everyday demands and expectations. To me it was clear that both of these aspects of her personality would have meant that the conduct of the officers would have escalated the situation as opposed to defusing it, and a lack of understanding of what remorse is, let alone how to express it, would be an expected characteristic within her neurodiverse framework. Therefore I instructed Sophie not to enter a plea, but asked the court to adjourn so a psychiatric assessment could be carried out.

The magistrates were unimpressed by this and kept pushing for Sophie to enter a plea. Every time I tried to argue the case, they were rude, disinterested and shut me down. The magistrates then refused to hear the case and we were told to come back later that day, when they wanted a guilty plea. I was threatened with contempt of court, and her horrified parents decided to reject my advice, and encouraged Sophie to plead guilty. She did so and, exactly as I had predicted, she was given a nine-month Referral Order (this means that the court referred her to a youth offending panel to find ways of addressing her offending). At least it was not a custodial sentence, but it still gave her a criminal record – purely because of her lack of remorse. It was highly frustrating and horrible that I had been so undermined, and once it was over I went into a side room and cried at the injustice of it all.

That was in 2018, which is far too recent for such a lack of understanding of Sophie's state of mind to be excusable. But I'd also like to hope that even in these few intervening years, the understanding of neurodiversity issues has come on a long way within the courtroom, and today Sophie's outcome might be different.

PTSD and Trauma

I struggle to think of any other situation in life where you make someone who has experienced a highly traumatic situation, and is perhaps suffering from PTSD, go over and over what has happened to them, questioning their experience and pulling apart their thoughts, decisions and feelings. In my opinion, the current legal system really is not trauma-informed, which, given that PTSD is the most common mental health condition I see among JfKL clients, is particularly shocking.

Imagine the scenario in which we are taking instructions from a child in an exploitation case. We have to go over every single traumatizing, awful detail and event that has happened to them in order to build up their defence and, as part of that process, we risk triggering them. Then we have to make them do it all over again in front of a court and jury, possibly at the risk of them not being believed. You wouldn't make someone who had suffered any other way during life go over and over it again. It can be incredibly damaging and triggering to the young person and impact on their recovery. I hate it.

All I can do is try to work in as trauma-informed a way as possible. So, for example, if there is a social services record that will assist, I will use that as a basis. I still have to check with the child that everything on there is correct, but it avoids pushing them into going over as much detail again. I will serve a schedule of these records as part of our evidence, and believe that it should be accepted by the prosecution that this young person has experienced this set of events. But because of the adversarial nature of our legal system, the prosecution inevitably won't accept anything that undermines their case, and cross-examination goes into overdrive. Unsurprisingly, our clients regularly talk about being triggered during this experience.

As our understanding of mental health grows, and it becomes clear the damage that giving evidence can cause, it is very apparent we are doing this all wrong. I believe that, especially when dealing with neurodiverse clients, we should take more of a lead from recent sex cases, in which prosecution witnesses who allege they are victims of crime give their account on a video-recorded interview that is played at the beginning of a court hearing as the evidence-in-chief, before they are cross-examined in person. If in some cases defendants were allowed to give evidence in this way, it would undoubtedly ease some of the pressure for them.

It is Not All on the CJS's Shoulders

It would be very easy to lay all the blame at the door of the police and the courts, but so many of these children and teenagers wouldn't even be in the courts if their issues had been caught and provided with support at an earlier stage. By the time a child is in the criminal justice system, chances are that far too much has already gone wrong in their life, and seeing all these missed opportunities is highly frustrating. The most important thing I want people to take away from reading this book is that these children should not be written off.

Access to psychological assessment in schools is obviously a massive issue – both getting it recognized when a child needs to have this in the first place, but also the length of time that children wait to get a Statement of Special Educational Needs. The fact that you either have to have a pushy parent or a pushy teacher in order to make that happen isn't the way it should be, but if you've got neither of those, then people just see the child's behaviour as 'problematic'.

The school system is focused on ensuring that if there are thirty pupils in the class, twenty-eight of them are not disrupted by two children. So for those two young people, the focus is on removing the disruption rather than on what's not working for them. It's hard to make the argument to the school that they've got a very important role to play in the lives of the two that are disrupting, when they are under their own financial/staffing/target pressures, and they've got another twenty-eight children to think about. But the trajectory that those two are likely – in the majority of cases – to take (you only have to look at the huge volume of young people like them who are excluded and then enter the criminal justice system) is a massive cost to society, and something different has to be on offer or available to schools for those two children.

Sadly, it isn't reflected in the availability of services to deal with it. A young person has to wait around eighteen months to be treated for mental health issues, and that is neither appropriate nor acceptable. They have lived through twelve years of austerity, with cuts in public services, a real lack of support, reduced access to youth and adolescent mental health services, a lack of referrals into mental health, or if they are referred, the waiting lists are long. Add into that everything to do with the trauma of Covid and lockdown, then as this generation is coming to adulthood, it feels like mental health is hitting crisis point.

At JfKL we were lucky enough to have received funding to have our own in-house therapist for twelve months, as unless children are acute, we can't get them any help. The attitude is often, 'Are you going to kill yourself or anyone else? If not, then you just have to get on with it.' However we have not been able to replace that funding now that the grant has ended, which was a real shame and meant we were again reliant on the slower referral system.

The absolute vulnerability that can accompany some degrees of autism led to the saddest incident we have experienced at JfKL. Andrew first came to us when he was sixteen years old. We had already worked with his brother, who had been exploited in county drug lines, but with Andrew it was a different situation: he had stolen a mobile phone from someone on his way to school, then felt bad and confessed to his mentor. They had reported him to the police, and he had been arrested. Over the next eighteen months we had further dealings with him for other crimes such as carrying a knife. There were a lot of questions around whether he, too, was being pulled into county lines. The Youth Offending Team he had been assigned to were seeing certain red flags: he would go missing from home for periods, and his mother, in despair, said to me that she was at her wit's end and was sure he was going to end up dead. Between him and his brother there were a lot of concerns.

We had a psychological assessment done, and it flagged up that Andrew had significant autistic traits. He seemed to find it particularly difficult to understand consequences, and his ability to consider risk was practically non-existent. It was disappointing that someone with such severe autistic traits hadn't been flagged up in the school system, and it felt that throughout his life not enough had been put in place to give him and his mother the support that was needed. His situation felt very bleak.

Then, in the summer, he and his brother went to a party in east London that was deemed an illegal rave. About 1.30 a.m. that night he was sitting on a bench, when someone drove by and started shooting. All the other kids ran for cover, or dived to the floor, but Andrew stood up and looked around to see what was happening. With that exact vulnerable streak that had worried me, that inability to instantly see the danger, he became a target, and was shot and killed.

The first I knew of it was a few hours later, when I got a call from his brother. He had been taken straight to the police station and questioned as a witness, and had just been dropped home.

I remember the moment so clearly as I came out of sleep to take in his words, the shock, confusion and sadness that overwhelmed me. His brother was in a panic, flitting from thought to thought: 'Will people try and get me too? Do I have to leave? What's going to happen?'

To my knowledge no one has ever been charged with Andrew's murder, although there was some talk of a fight on the estate the day before, in which someone had been assaulted with a hammer. Whether that was linked or not, with the shooting being some kind of botched revenge, I have no idea – although I know that Andrew and his brother had nothing to do with that fight.

It was certainly one of the most devastating sets of events I've seen at JfKL and really sent myself and the team reeling. A senseless death of a young man doing his best in a world that was just that bit harder for him to navigate than for others.

Psychosis

Psychosis among young people is, thankfully, still relatively rare, but it is a growing issue, and unfortunately can have extreme consequences. The charges tend to be on the more serious side – kidnap, threats to kill, possession of a firearm, intent to cause fear and violence … A teenager going through psychosis has effectively lost touch with reality. They might be hallucinating, hearing and seeing things, believing situations to exist that aren't true, and going through irrational, confused thoughts. These thoughts are 100 per cent real to them, and they genuinely believe them as fact, and that those who are thinking otherwise are the ones in the wrong.

Someone in the middle of a psychotic episode or breakdown can be quite terrifying to those around them, but they are also going through a terrifying internal struggle. I've had a client accused of criminal damage as she believed her neighbours were watching her, and in her mind she was trying to prevent that. Another client thought he was Moses. Unfortunately the signs are often there beforehand, but they aren't dealt with – and even once at the station they can be overlooked – as the case of Robbie shows.

Robbie was diagnosed with chronic fatigue and depression, and as he got older it really impeded on his mental health. Initially he was aware of this and had been asking for help for quite some time, but no one was taking him seriously, until it escalated. One day he went through a psychotic episode and grabbed a woman in the park, making threats to kill her. He was talking all sorts of gibberish, later confirmed that he was hearing voices and it was clear he was very mentally unwell. It was terrifying for the poor woman, and he was eventually arrested. In custody though, for some bizarre reason no one seemed to think a mental health professional needed to be called in.

He was sitting on the floor tearing up newspaper and placing the pieces in patterns, talking about the beauty of magic, and had ripped up a plastic cup he had been given and was cutting himself, smearing the blood across his forehead. When the duty solicitor arrived he took off his clothes during the consultation and was telling the solicitor not to worry, he was dead already. How did the solicitor or the police ever think that pressing ahead with this course of action was the right move? Robbie needed help.

I represented him at a later interview. Robbie said he felt he had been possessed by aliens during the incident and without a doubt felt that what he was doing at that time was the rational, correct course of action. Thankfully, we were able to get the case dropped and he became an in-patient with the local mental health services.

It was such an awful situation for both the victim and him, that could have been prevented had he got the help he needed when he had asked for it. And yet it was only once he was in the CJS that he was taken seriously. People shouldn't need to have committed a crime before their mental health needs are met; it should not be the only doorway into the mental health service.

I worked on one murder case with a young person who was a long-term client of JfKL, by which I mean he was a repeat offender of minor crimes, whom we had represented on several occasions. When he first came to us, he had just been diagnosed as autistic. I was shocked, as it was so apparent to me, but it had only come to light when he had appeared at court, and a member of the adolescent mental health team had seen all the signs, spoken to his mum, and made a referral.

That in itself angers me: up until then, no one in his life had taken the time to look at what was in front of them. One look at his school reports and the issues that were just written off as 'behavioural' ticked all the boxes of someone displaying traits of autism. Combined with that, he was very gifted mathematically, and had that been nurtured, this story might have a very different outcome. But as it was, nothing was done to create a place where he could thrive and reach his potential, and it was decided the school environment wasn't for him. He was excluded. Inevitably, he began associating with people who were getting into trouble, and soon we were taking regular calls about him – but half the time he was the victim, getting assaulted in the street, and half the time he was the perpetrator, such as being caught carrying a weapon, which he felt he needed to protect himself. It was a vicious circle.

He was getting mixed up in gangs and had an overwhelming need to fit in. It is quite common for children with autism to develop a street persona, as they watch how other people who seem to be respected in their area behave, then mimic that. He thought being bad is how you have to act, and how he would be accepted. And so, when postcode wars were starting to be discussed, he wrote on social media disrespecting another area. That lack of consequential thinking was exacerbated by his autism, and he was acting without really comprehending the risk he had placed himself in and the potential consequences. Then, of course, that heated things up tenfold and made him even more of a target. It was spinning out of control, a quickening downward spiral.

He would be on bail for an offence, then be attacked, then do something else himself – it was so chaotic. Then, thankfully, he was moved out of the area, but, as it turned out, that wasn't enough. When the call came in that he had been arrested for murder, I had a flood of emotions. I was angry and sad – at him, and for him, for the boy who had lost his life, and at the system that had done so little to stop it reaching this point. But one emotion I didn't feel was surprise. It wouldn't be quite right to call it a self-fulfilling prophecy, but it felt like this whole chain of complete failings had all led up to this one horrific, yet almost inevitable, event.

When I got to the police station, he was showing very little visible emotion. Where others might have been crying, scared or angry, he would have seemed to an outside eye to be completely cold, but to someone looking at him through an autistic filter, the signs were all there that it was the opposite. He had completely shut down, wasn't saying anything, couldn't eat and couldn't sleep, all indicators to me that he was very troubled.

It emerged that he had decided to go to Peckham that day to meet up with a friend, who later died in custody, and he had invited two other friends along from a youth club they were at together. He had also agreed to meet up with a girl in the postcode area he had criticized online – I think that while postcode rivalries seem to apply to boys, they are less relevant in the minds of girls, and their friendship had crossed that boundary, as it were. So my client got off the bus in that area, and the other three arrived in a cab from their youth club. As they got to the park there was a large group of lads there, as well as girls. It was never clear if it was a set-up, or coincidence, but when they entered the park, things escalated and one of the young men was stabbed several times. He died at the scene.

My client had run out of the park before the stabbing, but he was charged on a joint enterprise basis. On paper he didn't look great: he was the oldest in his group, and had previous convictions, so he was definitely viewed by the police as a troublemaker.

But trying to accuse a young person with autism of having the level of foresight that was needed in this situation was crazy; they were asking him to think about something so intangible, when he wouldn't have known what he was signing up to. The level of consequential thinking they were claiming he had, just wasn't there.

The jury ultimately accepted that there had been no planning for this on his part and acquitted him of joint enterprise GBH, and of joint enterprise murder. But they were aware of his previous and clearly thought there was no smoke without fire, so while they accepted that he didn't know of or intend for the outcomes, the jury must have felt there was guilt in there somewhere. He was convicted of manslaughter and is currently serving twelve years in prison.

Of all the cases I have taken on, this one really stands out for me, as it feels like a lot of the issues I've talked about in this book converged into that one grim and devastating day. But I can't help but feel that this young person, with different support for his autism, could have led such a different life, and I've found myself reflecting on it quite a lot since the case, and thinking about what we can all learn. An earlier diagnosis that could have kept him in school with the necessary support would have meant adults approaching him differently. He might then have been prevented from identifying himself as a 'bad kid', and could have focused on his aspirations and achievements with an understanding of his own struggle. It is speculation of course, but I can't help but feel sure that key diagnosis, and the resulting actions, would have led to a better life trajectory.

WHERE TO GET HELP:

- **The Mix:** Packed with articles and information about mental health for those under twenty-five, covering topics from anxiety and depression to self-care and counselling. There is also a phone line and an option for online chat. www.themix.org.uk

- **Papyrus:** A charity dedicated to the prevention of suicide and the promotion of positive mental health and emotional well-being in young people. They have various resources to download, plus a helpline, called HOPELINEUK. www.papyrus-uk.org

- **Samaritans:** A twenty-four-hour helpline for those who need someone to talk to. 116 123

CHAPTER 9

Is the Legal System Racist?

To cut straight to the chase, the simple and honest answer to this question, is unfortunately and unequivocally, 'Yes.' And I don't just mean one part of it. There is racism embedded in every area of the system, to varying degrees. From the police, to judges, from arrest to sentencing, racism unfortunately plays a part at every stage of the legal journey.

Statistically, as a black or other ethnic minority person, you are:

- (Still!) nine times more likely to be subjected to a stop and search than your white counterparts
- More likely to experience a violent arrest, with black children five times more likely to be tasered than white
- More likely to be remanded, once in court
- More likely to get a custodial sentence
- If ending up with a supervision order, more likely to be assessed by Youth Offending Teams to be high risk, and then go on to breach that order

- More likely to have a lower quality of supervision while on a court order, and have a less positive outcome

An incredibly depressing set of facts for every parent of a non-white child in the country – and for society as a whole.

It is a complex issue. People have written entire books just on this topic, so I'm not about to try to make this chapter an academic thesis on critical race theory, but it would be wrong not to acknowledge my experience of how racism plays out in the criminal justice system at the moment. I see it firsthand at work, whether it is black children who have been stopped and searched without reason, or those who get tougher sentences for the same offence as their white counterparts. In basic terms, the races most likely to get a tougher time in the criminal justice system are as follows:

- Being black has the most disproportionate impact on your treatment, followed by mixed race

- If you have an Asian ethnicity such as Indian or Pakistani, then there is the impact of the recent rise in Islamophobia, and for anything relating to issues such as terrorism or control orders, the impact is disproportionate

- The third group is Gypsy traveller and Roma communities, whose treatment within the criminal justice process also seems to be disproportionately tilted against them

Much of this was flagged up in the Lammy Review, published in 2017, which looked at the treatment and outcomes for black, Asian and minority ethnic people in the criminal justice system. The only area where the Lammy Review did not see a disproportionate impact on the lives of black children in the legal system, was in the charging decisions. However, one can only conclude that this was due to a lack of information, as the CPS commissioned its own study in 2023 that revealed that racialized defendants are more likely to be charged than their white counterparts.

The findings, described as 'troubling' by the CPS and experts, showed that defendants from mixed ethnic backgrounds are most likely to be charged, with 79.1 per cent of the suspects charged, almost ten percentage points higher than the rate of white British defendants charged. Black defendants had a charge rate of 76.2 per cent, which was seven percentage points higher than the rate of white British defendants; while 73.1 per cent of Asian defendants were charged, 3.5 percentage points above the white British rate. The racism continues in the court process, with a black person on a drugs charge 240 per cent more likely to receive a prison sentence than their white counterparts.

Racism is an area that really informs my work, but it can feel bleak at times. Being mixed race and having watched my dad's experience of the criminal justice system means I feel particularly close to it all. I find it difficult when presented with certain figures as they are so shocking, but that also fuels my passion to keep working and try to redress the balance. I want to give people faith, and there are times I need to restore my own, too, but it can be hard. If I have a run of cases where racism seems to be at the core, it can be draining, and I'll hit a wall; it can all feel too much.

The growth of the Black Lives Matter global movement, from its beginnings in 2013 and its further development after the murder of George Floyd in the US, seemed to have triggered a massive turning point for a lot of organizations. I remember feeling extremely frustrated and angry at the time, as it had taken a life-changing event such as the Covid pandemic for people to look outside their bubble and see what was going on. I have been witnessing and fighting against racism in the legal system for twenty years, but for so many people, it simply isn't something they see in their day-to-day lives. Suddenly, now that people were stuck at home without their usual distractions, and seeing this footage of a police officer literally murdering a black man played over and over, they were forced to confront what was happening. I fundamentally believe if there hadn't been a pandemic, there wouldn't have been the same outcry. That was what it took for people to realize the system wasn't fair.

The international outcry and call to action off the back of it, and the use of that campaign to penetrate companies and industries far and wide, meant that the impact of that one death, out of the many that there have been, was huge. In the year following it, I was asked to speak at events and contribute to guides, steering groups and all sorts of moves being taken to tackle the issue. Much of it still has to be actioned, and we need to see clear results, but at least there are now the resources that we can refer to openly in court.

Frustratingly, however, for some reason it doesn't seem to be filtering into the UK police forces. We have been challenging the system alongside police action lawyers and community groups, trying to hold officers to account for decades, doing our best to change the narrative for black children in the criminal justice system. But still, racialized children make up more than half the number of children in prisons and secure units, which is scandalous.

Racist Policing

The over-policing of black communities and black children has been well documented over the years, but there is often a false narrative that this is a thing of the past. Over-policing means that police have a disproportionate presence in certain communities, and come down more aggressively on lesser offences there than they do elsewhere, having a negative impact on the people living in those communities.

Stop and search is without a doubt still problematic among the black community. In 2020–1, there were 7.5 stop and searches for every 1,000 white people, compared with 52.6 for every 1,000 black people. Why is that? In theory, the police have to have a reason to stop a person, but I would say it is fairly open to interpretation. The officer has to have reasonable grounds to suspect you are carrying:

- illegal drugs

- a weapon

- stolen property

- something that could be used to commit a crime

They don't even need the reasonable grounds clause if a senior officer has given their approval, if they suspect that:

- Serious violence could take place

- You are carrying a weapon or have used one

- You are in a specific location or area

That last point is particularly vague to me. It is far too easy to tell a young person that there has been a robbery in the area and they fit the description. Whether it's true or not, a young person will probably never know. Often, young people will tell me they are stopped and asked to account for things such as who they are, why they are where they are, why they have each of their belongings, or to prove that the mobile phone in their hand is theirs. No police officer should be doing that without reasonable grounds, and yet it still seems to be very common, and happening disproportionately often to black children.

Josh was out on his electric scooter when police jumped out of the back of a van, stopped him and asked him what he was doing. They asked if he had anything on him that he shouldn't, and he said no, but they decided to search him anyway. What grounds they had to do so is questionable to say the least. They got him into the van, a pretty intimidating situation for a seventeen-year-old who, until then, had had no dealings with the police. They asked to see what he had, and he pulled out an Oyster card that he had recently found. Having been told that you could get a £5 reward if you handed a card in, that was his plan, but he was worried about saying to officers that it wasn't his. The officer noticed that the card had a different name on it, and when he called him up on it, in a panic Josh said, 'Oh, it's my cousin Jacob's.' The police then went through the contacts on his phone, found Jacob and called him, and worked out that it wasn't his Oyster card either.

So Josh was arrested on a charge so ridiculous, I had to go back through my case notes to remember what it was: possession of an article for use in fraud. They managed to find an offence that vaguely matched up, and one that I had never come across before.

The explanation was so simple and innocent, and Josh had an exemplary record, yet they still felt the need to try to find something to justify their stop and search. He was taken to the police station, and his dad went down too. By the time I got involved, I was furious. Sadly his dad, while being supportive of his son, was almost resigned to it: this is something that black boys just have to deal with, he said, utterly depressing me. But I was outraged.

I wrote a prepared statement setting out what happened and the level of intimidation Josh felt, and we went into interview. And then, thank goodness for a sensible officer. He listened to me read the statement, then turned the tape off, and in front of the boy and his dad, said: 'It is days like this that make me ashamed to be a police officer.'

The fact that he had been stopped in the first place, intimidated the way he was, and that this farcical charge had been dreamt up, was nothing more than racist. The officer continued, 'I'm going to walk out of here and throw this case in the bin. There will be no further action.'

It was a positive – but also the only sensible – outcome. And actually, whether he realized it or not, that police officer may well have changed the narrative for that young person going forward, in terms of his expectations of the police. It's just a shame that officers like him are so rare. Sadly this alternative view is rarely presented to young black people, but at the same time those are the moments that keep me going, those opportunities where I can make a difference, and also see a difference in the behaviour of others. All too often, however, in the police station particularly, I am left feeling frustrated rather than inspired.

Another recent client of JfKL, Matthew was stopped out on his electric bike, quite an expensive model, but lawfully paid for from his part-time job. With no good reason, the police challenged him with the idea that the bike wasn't his, asking where he had got it from. Things escalated and Matthew was subjected to a violent arrest and restraint, and was charged with assaulting a police officer.

At the first appearance the prosecutor told us that they had reviewed the Body Worn camera footage, and there had been no good reason for the client to have been stopped or then charged, and they weren't proceeding with the case. Off the record, they accepted that, essentially, the only reason they could see for the set of circumstances, was racist behaviour by the police. As no further action was being taken, the CPS refused to serve us with the footage.

The JfKL solicitor who looked after the case was furious, and wanted our client to take civil action, as there were such good grounds to do so, and the footage, which would have to be disclosed in a civil action, would have supported his case. But Matthew's take on it was, 'What is the point? I'm just going to be harassed even more by the local police if I do that,' as he had seen this happen to a friend in a similar situation. I can't blame Matthew, but so the cycle continues, and the police get away with it.

It is a common response. I think people see racist policing as an American issue, but to me the only real difference is the day-to-day officers policing the streets here don't have guns, so the outcome tends to be less dramatic. However when it comes to tasers, excessive restraint, etc., we are right up there on the issue of racist behaviour from police. Recently, in 2023, freedom of information data extracted from the police by the independent investigative journalism unit Liberty Investigates found that over the last six years the Metropolitan Police had authorized the potential use of batons only at black-led events such as the Notting Hill Carnival and Black Lives Matter protests. What concerns me is the growing potential for police in this country to be armed in the future. At the moment, it is only certain officers who carry guns – firearms officers who have been specially trained – but I can't say I am comfortable with even some police being armed in this way. You only need to look at the recent case of Chris Kaba, who was unarmed when he was shot through the front window of his car in London.

The officer has since been charged, leading to dozens of Met officers handing in their firearm permits in protest that they felt undermined. I await the outcome, but it seems to be inevitable: when police officers are armed, black people are killed.

There is one advantage to social media though, which is that it has resulted in the general public becoming more active citizens. They will see something happening on the street that they think is wrong, record it, put it up on social media and it goes viral, thus holding people to account more readily and preserving evidence of wrongdoing that could be invaluable later. There are lawyers and community groups who are picking up on these things and running with them, creating a media frenzy and public outcry which forces action to be taken. Just this week I saw a boy with a huge black eye after a police arrest, and a seventy-year-old man who was clearly assaulted during a stop and search. I don't know if the Independent Office for Police Conduct (IOPC) is busier as a direct result of social media activity – complaints did go up by 8 per cent in 2022–3 compared to the year before – but it certainly feels as if there is more of an alliance among the general public, which is encouraging. People calling out this kind of behaviour and being willing to support others is exactly what we need to see, so that society as a whole can hold the police to account.

Who are the IOPC?

The Independent Office for Police Conduct (IOPC) oversees the police complaints system in England and Wales. They describe themselves thus:

> We investigate the most serious matters,
> including deaths following police contact, and
> set the standards by which the police should
> handle complaints. We use learning from our
> work to influence change in policing. We are
> independent, and make our decisions entirely
> independently of the police and government.

The IOPC replaced the Independent Police Complaints Commission (IPCC) in 2018, after various issues including accusations of favouritism in that organization's decision-making towards the police, complaints being rejected despite overwhelming evidence, and indifference and rudeness to complainants. A 2012 Parliamentary enquiry deemed the IPCC: '... woefully underequipped and hamstrung in achieving its original objectives. It has neither the powers nor the resources that it needs to get to the truth when the integrity of the police is in doubt.' I have no doubt the lack of accountability, particularly within the Metropolitan Police, has been bolstered by the inadequacy of the IOPC.

However, with good civil lawyers, it is possible to take on the system and win. One client had a recording of an officer being openly racist to him, and while the officer was charged, he was subsequently acquitted at trial by the jury. (As a side note, I do find that juries seem reluctant to find police officers guilty.) My client hired civil lawyers and the recording was so blatant, that when they took it to the IOPC, this organization took a different stance on what had happened. The officer was sacked from his job, and my client was awarded £20,000 compensation.

We don't take on civil cases such as these, as it is a different discipline to criminal law and you need to have an Action Against Public Authorities contract with the Legal Aid

Agency. But we will always put any of our clients in contact with those who do take this action and encourage them to go for it when we can see there is a clear case to be answered – which, far too often, I'm afraid there is.

Reasonable Force and the Right to Silence During Arrest

The question of what is reasonable force during an arrest is such a grey area. I tend to turn it round, as working out what *unreasonable* force looks like is perhaps easier. Unless the person being arrested has shown themselves to be especially violent or dangerous, I would take issue with any marks being left on them by the arrest. This is particularly true when it comes to a child. Unless they are a genuine risk to themselves or others, I would not be happy about any cuts or bruises caused by an arrest. Sadly, I have seen children with bruises the shape of a boot mark on their body or with severe cuts on their wrists due to handcuffs being too tight. In these circumstances I will always take photographs of their injuries to preserve evidence that can be used later on. I would also be keen to see the Body Worn camera footage in these cases. Police need to switch on the camera, generally pinned on the torso of their uniform, whenever they are making an arrest, and the courts take a dim view of it if an officer claims to have forgotten to do so, or if the footage has been lost.

Unconscious Bias

I hear the phrase 'unconscious bias' bandied about a lot these days. I don't dispute that it exists – all of us will have biases to some degree about certain sets of people. But it has become a sweeping term that is almost used as an excuse, meaning that people don't confront the issues that come with it, and that isn't acceptable. It has become a way for people to say, 'Well, it wasn't my fault, I'm not inherently racist, it was my subconscious doing it', as though your subconscious is not a part of you. The phrase has become watered down, making it almost palatable.

- **What unconscious bias is:** having a view that you aren't consciously aware of about a set of people, but a view that may impact your thoughts or behaviour
- **What unconscious bias is not:** an excuse to accept lazy stereotyping, without educating yourself, or an explanation to hide behind for racist behaviour

There are studies around darkness of skin, and unfortunately blackness is still something that for some people is automatically associated with the negative. There is still an underlying expectation that black children will be worse behaved. Isn't that an awful thing to assume – that a child, simply because of the colour of skin they were born with, is more likely to be bad? You would hope that our police officers would be above that, though, wouldn't you? That they would have challenged themselves over stereotypes and educated themselves into the reality that we should all be viewed the same in the eyes of the law.

But if a police officer perceives a black child who is doing nothing more than walking down the street as a potential threat and arrests or searches him, the obvious question is why? People shrug it off as an unconscious bias that black children are more likely to be involved in criminal behaviour, but that is purely and simply a deep-rooted racism and should be called out as such.

As I said before, we all have our own unconscious biases in the way that we see things, whether related to race or otherwise. They can come from life experiences, something our family or friends have passed on to us, or something soaked up from our culture or society. But that doesn't mean it is something that should be accepted. Challenging yourself as to where the root and truth of these biases come from can really help to change them.

A good example would be in how we assess risk within Youth Offending Teams, units that are like the probation service but created to deal with children. They are made up mainly of social workers who are responsible for supervising children on court orders or in the criminal justice system – as opposed to social workers who are dealing with looked-after children or child protection.

If you remember from Chapter 1, I was a Youth Offending Team officer in my days before JfKL. We used a scoring tool called Asset that aimed to work out how a child's future might look in terms of risk – for example, their risk of reoffending, or causing harm to the public. But the assessment itself was based on Eurocentric ideas of what would constitute a risk, and unless the assessor had that awareness, it could be problematic. At first glance you might think there was no sign of any bias, but Asset placed a lot of emphasis on personal judgement, which was inevitably based on a very traditional British sense of culture and norms. In the past, this might have meant that a child from a single-parent home might have been assessed to not be able to achieve as highly as one in which the parents were together. Now, of course, single-parent homes are so common that people know not to make that judgement, but there are still plenty of other biases in its place.

So, for example, a child who is eating with his hands could be seen as living in a neglectful family set-up, where he hasn't been taught to use cutlery, whereas in some cultures it would be viewed as the cleaner and more appropriate way to eat.

With my background, I know that multiple generations of a family living together isn't a sign of a troubled home life, but is perfectly normal in a black Caribbean community. My understanding of ways of living that would be protective to a young person's life within the context of their race and culture, might be more competent than a white member of staff from an entirely different background. Without that cultural sensitivity, the assessor might perceive situations and make judgments that would have an impact on that child's future. It is a fact that black children will score more highly in those assessments and be expected to do more to prove they are rehabilitating, than their white counterparts.

The assessor believes they are being as fair and helpful as they can be, but their scoring and decisions might be tainted by the ideas and beliefs in their subconscious. It is a subtle difference to the way someone perceives a scenario, but I think training and education to ensure a person is alive to the idea that they might be perceiving situations with a 'white' mind, can make a difference, although this of course relies on a person being open to considering that this is a possibility. Unfortunately what happens to black children within the legal system makes it clear that a lot of people aren't working hard enough to make that change.

Asset has since been replaced by AssetPlus, a system that has taken into account new developments in assessment practice, including ideas about the perceptions of the users but I am unaware as to whether the objectivity of assessments has improved. Developing the cultural awareness of those making assessments is more likely to achieve the desired outcome.

The Adultification of Black Boys

If you come across a large, well-built teenager in the street, in a fight with a scrawny, slight boy, chances are, you will assume the larger teen started the fight. Who knows whether you will be right or not, but it all boils down to perceived vulnerability. Most people equate size with strength and power, and in terms of children, there is an assumption that when they are larger in size, they are also older, and therefore more responsible.

Of course this often isn't the case – I know if I look at my teenage son and his friendship group, the smallest boy, who at an initial glance you would perhaps pick out as the most vulnerable, would definitely be the most resilient of them all, whereas the stockiest boy has the least confidence.

How we define vulnerability is very important, as it is a big factor in the criminal justice system. Vulnerability among children is seen as a mitigating factor in the eyes of the law. If the Youth Offending Team say a child is vulnerable, that child is less likely to be remanded in custody, or may end up in a secure children's home rather than prison. But, with that in mind, we need to acknowledge that black and mixed-race boys often grow faster and look older than their white peers. As a result of that – and a number of other factors I'll come back to – they are often not really viewed as children, and are therefore not afforded the notions of innocence and vulnerability. This happens in many situations within the education system, social services and mental health services, but particularly in the criminal justice system.

The term adultification has become commonly used in recent years to describe this idea of black children being treated as older than their white peers. One of the UK's leading safeguarding experts, Jahnine Davis, specializes in adultification. She says: 'We have been talking about the adultification of Black children for many years, but now we have a word to frame those experiences.' But as she explains, it is not just a case of physical growth:

> Historically Black people have been
> dehumanized and devalued, perceived as
> less than. When we look at various racialized
> stereotypes which are rooted in slavery, Black
> children aren't afforded innocence. We need to
> acknowledge racism exists, then start exploring
> the way we safeguard – or don't – Black children.

> Ultimately the impact means there is a
> dereliction of our safeguarding duty. It means
> we are less likely to provide the support
> that Black children, and all children should
> receive because we cast them aside, erase
> their vulnerability, and instead increase their
> culpability and see them as undeserving victims
> rather than children who should be safeguarded
> and have the right to be protected.

I regularly come across this kind of adultification. One day I was called to a police station for a case in which a black boy had been accused of sexual touching at school. In consultation, he took off his jacket and was wearing a tight hoodie, and I was immediately struck by how skinny he was.

We went into the interview, and the officer kept saying: 'Well, you're a big guy aren't you?' 'Well, you know that you are a tall and big guy?' I was confused: what was she seeing in front of her? After the fourth comment I became angry: it was as if the officer wanted to create the narrative that this boy was a large, predatory man on the interview tape.

In the end I intervened and said: 'Sorry, I don't understand. He's not taller than other sixteen-year-olds, he's got a really slight build, I don't understand why you would keep saying that, other than racism.'

Of course, she said it had nothing to do with that and responded, 'I didn't mention the word black.' I replied: 'Well, what are you seeing in your mind and trying to register on this tape? As I only see a slightly built boy.'

She didn't mention his build again, nor did it come up in the second interview. It was frustrating as it simply wasn't relevant. But this was in a village in Buckinghamshire, where he was one of very few black boys in his school, with the reports of sexual touching made by middle-class white girls. Regardless of his guilt or innocence, it felt as though the police were taking the lazy route of trying to build up a stereotypical narrative of a large, predatory black man. A very dangerous strategy, when this can impact on decisions on how the case moved forward – and what future this boy faced.

The term 'adultification' isn't popular with everyone though, as, a little like unconscious bias, it can be misused almost as a way to excuse racism. You can find that officers are comfortable saying: 'I may have adultified these children in the system, as I see black children as older, but it wasn't racist.' There's no excuse for it though, it is not a get-out clause. For me adultification and racism go hand in hand.

Is it the Same for Black Girls?

The adultification of black girls tends to be less focused on physical size and strength, but they face their own set of problems. In particular, there is a perceived idea that they can't ever be naive and vulnerable, but are always streetwise and tough. They are also painted as rude and hypersexualized. I often see this misrepresentation directed towards black girls who have been sexually exploited – there is more chance of a prosecution lawyer painting them as a kind of Lolita-style, sexualized child who has 'consented' to the abuse, rather than being a victim.

That same idea of 'being tough' is believed to be behind the horrifying figures around the deaths of black women during pregnancy or childbirth. Black women are four times more likely to die during this period than white women, and the chances of them experiencing a difficult birth are much higher. There are various contributing factors, but one of them is thought to be the perception that black women have a higher pain threshold, so they are denied pain relief, or their concerns aren't listened to in labour. This way of thinking is rooted in slavery, and micro-aggressions such as these can have dire consequences.

We had a case of a girl in Brighton who had been reported missing with a friend. They were stopped by police and the interaction became fraught, and when the policeman was restraining her, she says he was calling her a n*gger. She was charged with assaulting the officer, but when we asked for the Body Worn camera footage, we were told it had gone missing. To me, if anything pointed to the fact that what she was claiming was true, it was that. It just felt like such a case of the police protecting themselves rather than holding themselves accountable. Eventually the case got dropped, but not before a pretty traumatic time all round.

I had another client, a black girl, who had a long history of being sexually and criminally exploited. This time she was caught when she was forced to take drugs into a prison by her exploiters. Social services acknowledged her vulnerability to some degree, but the officer involved didn't take that stance – instead she was adamant it was a lifestyle choice. Would she have thought the same if my client had been a white girl?

It Happens to Me, Too

One Sunday morning I received a call about a boy who had been brought into the police station for interview in relation to an allegation of rape. It was the first time the client had been in trouble, and he had been personally referred to me, so while I try to keep weekends for family life, I do at times inevitably end up taking on work that feels particularly important. So, I put on my suit and headed off to the appointment. Weekends can be a bit more relaxed in terms of what people wear within the profession – you aren't expected to be as suited and booted out of hours – but because of the seriousness of the allegation, it felt appropriate.

I got to the station, and found his mum waiting for me. She was a white, middle-class woman, dressed casually in jeans, trainers, and a purple T-shirt.

The custody sergeant came over to us as we stood discussing the situation and, speaking directly to me, asked, 'Are you mum?'

I was dumbstruck at the assumption. Why would you think that I, a mixed-race woman in a suit, would be the mother, and the white woman in weekend casuals would be the lawyer? It was such a stark comparison, and said so much about the role the officer thought someone like me was more likely to be playing in that situation.

Unfortunately, I experience this a lot. An assumption that I am the social worker or part of the Youth Offending Team, but never the lawyer. I rarely call it out, although I hope that the tone of my reply at least makes it clear that I'm not impressed. I do think the next generation are better at confronting the subtle, everyday racism that many before felt they just had to accept. I know some lawyers have spoken quite openly about the assumption that they are the defendant. One such person is Alexandra Wilson, who in 2020 wrote a book called *In Black and White*. She was very vocal on social media about experiencing this kind of treatment, and has done a great job in shining a light on the issues.

It says so much about people's perception of what a lawyer should be. They just don't think a mixed-race woman (even with fair skin) with curly hair is the image of who should be fighting a case. Society is programmed to see a smart, well-spoken, forceful white man in a suit as the image of the ultimate lawyer. I don't know whether the blame for this skewered thinking lies with the media, or TV shows, or simply the lawyers who have come before, but it is systemic.

We even see this biased thinking with our young people who are involved with JfKL, no matter what race they are themselves. We have young people who work with us in a range of ways, whether that is through campaigning, volunteering, or just feeding in thoughts and experiences to help us keep learning and developing. We have a panel of young people involved whenever we are interviewing for a role, as their feedback on future staff is important to us. But we have found they are more likely to give us negative feedback on the black interviewees than the white, via quite vague, unsubstantiated, negative comments, such as:

- 'I don't think they somehow looked professional enough,'
- 'They don't look like they should earn as much money as you are offering.'

It is as though in their minds somehow this person doesn't match up with their image of a successful lawyer – because they aren't white.

We sometimes see the same issue with the parents of our clients – an inbuilt idea of what a lawyer should be – and we don't always match up to that. Not too long ago we had one client's father telephone us to request that we didn't assign a black lawyer to his child, he only wanted a white lawyer. He was a black man himself, but in his words: 'He's not won any of his cases with black lawyers, so I want a white lawyer as the system works for white people.' So sad and demoralizing to hear.

I'm frequently asked why I choose to work in a profession that so actively discriminates against people of colour and women. I have thought about it, and about the best way to react to those who do discriminate and to make a difference.

Ultimately, I think that the only way to change the system is to work from within it. I can feel completely beaten down at times, but it is the other moments, when you make a difference to a child's life, that lift me back up.

Add Sexism into the Mix ...

There is definitely a degree of sexism at play too, at times. People think you have to go in all gung-ho, cocky and aggressive to win a case, and the stereotypical expectation is that those characteristics are more likely to be found in a male. Although ironically, if you want to stick with stereotypes, I think a softer 'female' approach actually works better with children. I try to take quite a maternal approach with my clients, constantly aware of their well-being, and think about how I can explain things to them in a simple, comprehensible language, so they understand what is happening to them. Plain, considerate English is much more conducive to building a relationship and rapport with a child, so being much less obviously 'legal' is a deliberate decision. But I am well aware that sometimes I have parents watching me, thinking: 'She's not using legal jargon, I don't think she knows what she is talking about.' They think I am a soft, inexperienced female, and I can practically see the cogs whirring as they compare that image to their preconceived idea of what a professional lawyer should be like.

Combine the sexism and racism and I definitely feel the impact at times. I've had parents being really difficult, despite the fact I have been connecting with their child, have found all the right routes into the case, and been making the best legal representations possible. But still they are questioning me, as though waiting for me to make a mistake so they can transfer the case to someone else. At those times I naturally begin to think that it is based on a perception that I am not going to do as good a job as a white man. I don't match up to their idea of professionalism and success, so I'm starting from a losing position in their eyes.

Statistically, in 2022 18 per cent of solicitors working in the UK were black, Asian or of another ethnic minority, a slight increase on recent years, and 53 per cent were women, although the seniority gap between the sexes was still described as 'significant'. So things are slowly getting better, and representation onscreen is helping in that – whether it is Jessica Pearson running the law firm in *Suits*, or Jax Stewart in *Reasonable Doubt*, we are seeing black women at the top of the legal game. The same thing is happening more and more in real life, and that is the only way we are going to move forward.

What About Judges?

I don't honestly think I have experienced different treatment from a magistrate because of my race or sex. Perhaps because in the magistrates' courts they come across so many different solicitors on a daily basis, with a constant stream of cases coming through their doors, that one is just the same as the next.

It can be a slightly different situation in Crown Court though, which I can only put down to the more traditional, old-fashioned environment. I was watching a case in the Crown Court once, in which the prosecutor was a white, male barrister, and the defence lawyer was a black, female solicitor-advocate. She was doing a good job, making well-reasoned arguments with zero errors in her case, but the difference in the way the judge spoke to her, as opposed to the prosecutor, was stark in its comparison. The rude and dismissive way he approached his interaction with her was so bad, that I actually found it quite distressing to sit and watch. And, of course, my mind was questioning the reason. Perhaps they had history prior to this case, or perhaps it was a kind of snobbery where the judge felt someone not coming up through the traditional route shouldn't be taken seriously. But inevitably I ended up considering the option that he had a problem with her being a black woman in that role. I – and she – will never know. But whatever the reason, it represented everything that is wrong with this traditional profession that is protected for the white male.

I believe it is extremely important for children of colour to see representation across the board. For a child, seeing someone with the same colour skin as them in all sorts of roles, helps them to believe that they can do whatever they want to do, and there are no limitations because of their race. It is also important in terms of the lawyers connecting with the child. The Lammy Review flagged up a huge issue with people saying they didn't trust their lawyer, and if they don't trust you, then they won't tell you everything – and how are you going to get their case across to the best of your ability without all the facts? If you can't advise them correctly, it impacts how the case moves forward, and has a knock-on effect on the whole system. In some ways the colour of my skin can be helpful with children. Because I am mixed-race, people see me as 'other'. They may not realize that I am black Caribbean and white mixed as I am very fair skinned, and they often think I am Moroccan, or Arabic. I find that often those children instinctively trust me a little more, as in their mind it separates me from the predominantly white legal system they are involved in.

Other Factors

There are so many components that play into the courtroom narrative. The language used, for example, is one crucial element. It is more likely that a group of black boys in court together for a crime will be described as a gang, and they are three times as likely to be convicted under joint enterprise as a result. That same language is much less likely to be used for a group of white boys. We must be more alive to that language and the narrative that is being allowed to exist, and then challenging that. Saying to people, 'Check yourself: actually, look at the sentencing guidelines. Why are you giving them harsher sentences?' Or challenging the Youth Offending Team: 'Why are you viewing this person as high risk, and not offering them a bail package?'

You have to remind people, and create an alternative narrative – after all, that's what we are all about as lawyers: presenting events in different lights. You will be doing that with your client anyway, spotlighting certain aspects, and stopping the other lawyer spotlighting other bits. But you have to work harder when representing black children, as there are so many more factors to consider. Not only are you reminding everyone in the room that they are dealing with a child, but you also need to challenge all the other stereotypical and sometimes racist perceptions at play.

We now have tools to help us. For example, after the Lammy Review you are allowed to say in open court, 'As sentencers you are more likely to send him to prison because of the colour of his skin', to remind the judge and jury of their responsibilities, and make them aware of that. But not everyone likes to hear it.

I was part of an advisory group set up by Dr Laura Janes at the Howard League for Penal Reform, who created a guide for antiracist lawyers, and when I recently uploaded it at a sentence hearing as part of the evidence, the judge was really offended. He made a point of saying he wasn't impressed, wouldn't be reading it, and that judges were trained in 'that sort of thing'. But it is tough, because the statistics say otherwise, so as a lawyer it is your job to call it out in court, challenge it at every step and respond to things in a professional manner. Holding people accountable for their actions when it comes to racial prejudices is something I see as a crucial part of my job.

Equally, other judges have been much more receptive. One colleague had a judge again bring up the fact that the guidelines had been uploaded – but this time it was to thank her, and say that it had been very helpful.

When you look at the people upholding the law, statistics in 2022 showed that ethnic minority individuals made up 16 per cent of barristers, 18 per cent of solicitors and 9 per cent of Chartered Legal Executives, though representation generally fell with increasing experience and seniority.

In terms of the judiciary, the percentages are increasing, but are still not yet representative of society. Crucially, though, we need to stop here and think: even if the statistics were 'representative' in terms of numbers, would they truly reflect the interests of those accused? I've been in front of many black judges, who are completely unable to relate to my young black clients in any way. If you are black, but have been to private school and had a very middle- or upper-class lifestyle, then the colour of your skin may not help you relate to my client. Classism is also at play, so we need to be thinking more about the lived experience and understanding of these communities, rather than just a shared skin tone.

This same idea of classism can be seen in terms of education. The better a child is doing in mainstream education, the better a chance they have of being viewed favourably in court. They are often seen by judges or magistrates as having made an error of judgement with their crime but that, given a chance, they will be able to put themselves back on the right track. Statistically, well-educated children get more lenient sentences. So while representation is important, just putting more black faces into the space isn't necessarily going to help, it is about that real understanding.

That idea of traditional education is very much a middle-class ideal, so, as a lawyer, you find yourself having to frame your mitigation for your client around that. For a child who has taken a different route, or who isn't particularly academic, it feels as though you need to explain why, or give that some kind of validity. Then you may have a client who has dropped out of education all together, and you are really struggling to create a narrative around them that would be accepted in court. Ultimately, they are seen as a bit feral, and excluded through their own fault.

A lot of lawyers will only meet their clients on the day of their first court appearance – something that really shocks a lot of parents. They ask them the basic questions to get some background: 'Who do you live with? What do you do with yourself?', etc. These are all topics the lawyers know the court will be interested in. But if you come from a broken home, live in relative poverty, and are out of education, it is like a tick list of everything the courts hate. The space isn't really given to tell the young person's story.

We try to do it differently, dig a bit deeper and really get to the bottom of what has informed the person they are. It might be that they ended up dropping out of school as they are a carer, and what they have been through has given them a lot of resilience and potential in a different way. We try to perceive strength in areas outside the obvious. Because if the middle-class ideals limit even the questions that representatives ask of children, then you have no chance of giving someone from a working-class background a crack at defending themselves anything like on a par with their middle-class counterparts.

Sentencing

It was in Crown Court, too, that I came across a very clear example of racism in sentencing.

We have small wins all the time when it comes to the treatment of young people by the police – children who have challenged them by taking civil action or going to the IOPC and getting compensation, or magistrates who have stated in court that the behaviour of the police in a certain situation can't be described as anything short of racist. But despite the findings of the Lammy Review, and feelings I have about a bias in sentencing at times, it is often hard to assess whether it is racism, or some other aspect that has come into play in certain cases.

But not so with this one – or two, really, as it was comparing two extremely similar cases that was a red flag to me. There are normally so many different factors from case to case, that any discrepancies can be put down to something else. So when this one happened across my desk, I couldn't believe my eyes at the blatant imbalance.

One summer, in the gap between sixth form and university, two friends, Shaun and Junaid, went to a Festival near Winchester, Hampshire. Along with their friends, they agreed that they wanted to take drugs at the event, and these two bought them to sell to a select bunch of their mates so that they could fund their weekend. I'm not saying this is acceptable behaviour, but the same thing happens up and down the country all the time, within hundreds of groups of mates – they all decide they want in, and one or two people effectively become mini dealers to their friends for that night.

Both boys were caught at the festival, and faced the same charge of possession with intent to supply, but as they had been stopped separately at the event, they were tried separately in court. Shaun, who was white, was given a community order; Junaid, who was black, was sentenced to three years in jail.

Neither boy had been in trouble before, both had a place at university waiting for them, and their academic potential was on a par. On paper, they should have been treated the same. The first Junaid's mum knew of it was when he called her from prison, as he had kept it secret when on bail, hoping she would never need to know. She spoke to his old school, and a concerned teacher, who was aware of the work of one my colleagues who happened to have a child attending the same school, advised her to get in touch.

I felt really shocked as I sat reading through the papers, and couldn't see how anything other than racism could have caused such a disparity in the sentencing. So JfKL took it to appeal, a barrister agreed to work for free, making submissions on the basis of the Lammy Review, and the sentence was reduced by eight months, effectively almost freeing Junaid as the process had lasted so long. The phrasing from the Court of Appeal didn't acknowledge it was racist, simply stating: 'We accept his personal characteristics were not given sufficient credit.' For me, that avoided the issue, but it was the first time I had seen such a direct comparative example, and the messaging was clear to me. As a side note, Junaid was able to pick up his university place a year on, is doing well with his studies, and has even spent time working for JfKL during his holidays.

What Can I Do About it?

It is a good idea for parents and children – not just black and mixed-race children, but all children – to be aware of their rights, especially when it comes to stop and search and how you should be treated by the police. So a key step everyone should take is to be as educated as possible about what is acceptable treatment and what is not. But at the same time, much as it pains me to say it, sadly I wouldn't necessarily encourage the child to challenge any of their treatment with the officer at the time, because you don't know what could happen. If they are perceived to be non-compliant or difficult, the situation might escalate and they could be physically restrained, tasered or worse. I have told my own children this, so that while they have an understanding of their rights, they know to go along with the situation at the time, and we will deal with any issues after. It is a case of not encouraging your children into a potentially inflammatory situation alone and without your protection – but if there has been an issue with their treatment, be proactive about it afterwards.

If you think you have been a victim of racism at the hands of the law, the first thing to do is log a complaint. You are entitled to get the stop and search records for your child from a police station, if they weren't given a copy on the street. That way you can see if there is a particular policing strategy happening, or can monitor if a particular officer is targeting your child. Then, enlist the support of a police actions lawyer who can preserve evidence for you such as custody records along with custody and Body Worn footage.

If they are called in for further questioning, make sure your children are represented at the police station. As I explained earlier, this is such a huge failing by so many people, but it is a fact that black people have less faith in the legal system, so think that advising their child to just say 'No comment' to every question is the safest route. The reality is that in some cases this can lead to escalation and charges. If the children were represented, everyone could understand whether there is any legal basis for the arrest, there would be a lot more scrutiny and advice, you would be in a much more secure place from the off, and the chance of ensuring that, if there was an offence, it is diverted out of the court process, is much increased.

Ultimately, there is a lot of information out there – the way our system works means these damning reports have to be published, and websites such as www.gov.uk contain many of them. So research, arm yourself with knowledge, know your rights, hold people to account, and get help from the places that exist for exactly that reason.

WHERE TO GET HELP

I'd like parents to take away from this that there are people out there who can help them challenge these decisions or take action:

- StopWatch – support and advice for those affected by stop and search: www.stop-watch.org
- Unjust – a not-for-profit organization challenging discriminatory policies and practices within policing and the legal system: www.unjust.org.uk
- Bhatt Murphy Solicitors – www.bhattmurphy.co.uk
- Bindmans law firm – www.bindmans.com
- Hodge Jones & Allen Solicitors – www.hja.net

CHAPTER 10

Is a Seventeen-Year-Old an Adult or a Child?

When Carrlean's son didn't come home one evening, she thought the worst. Although he was seventeen years old, Hughes had always let her know when he planned to stay out late, so she began ringing round his friends and local hospitals, her panic growing with each negative response. Unbeknown to her, Hughes was sitting in a cell, having been arrested on suspicion of robbery while on board a bus in south London. But despite still being a child, the police only had a duty to inform an appropriate adult, such as a parent, about the arrest of anyone under the age of sixteen, so Carrlean was kept in the dark.

The first his mother knew about her son's whereabouts was when police officers turned up to search the house, four hours after his arrest. She rushed down to the station but was refused a chance to see Hughes, who by then, adamant he was innocent and confused about his legal rights, had turned down access to a duty solicitor. When he was finally released twelve hours later, Carrlean and Hughes were so angry and upset about the experience they had gone through, they contacted

JfKL, convinced his treatment must have been illegal. We explained to them that it wasn't, but we agreed with them: it was a strange lacuna in the law that saw him viewed as a child in most other aspects of legislation, but not this.

So, while the charges of robbery against Hughes were dropped when he was found to be innocent, Shauneen Lambe, my fellow founder of Just for Kids Law, decided to take the case to judicial review, with the main aim of tackling this loophole.

A judicial review is a court proceeding in which a judge looks at the lawfulness of a process, or the way in which a decision has been made by a public body – in this case the police. As our campaign developed and we began looking for evidence and examples of lived experiences, word spread about the changes we were looking to make in the law. Other parents came forward with similar stories, including two particularly tragic cases. For the parents in these examples it hadn't just been a night of worry, but had turned into a lifetime of sadness: in separate cases, their sons had committed suicide, terrified of telling their parents of their arrests, and worried how it would impact on their futures.

Edward had been about to head off to teach at a summer camp in America when he was arrested for possession of cannabis worth just 50p. Aware that a drugs conviction would most likely prevent him from travelling from his home in Didsbury to the States for his new job, and convinced his future was ruined, he took his own life, two days after receiving an order to appear in court.

Joe was arrested for drink-driving. Crippled by the idea that he had disappointed his family, he also took his own life, using a shotgun from the family farm in Stockport. Speaking at the time, Joe's mum, Jane, said: 'We really do believe that if Joe had been treated as a child when in custody, if he had the chance to ring us … if he had our help and support, he would still be with us today.'

Think back to the discussion earlier in the book about brain development in teenagers, and their lack of foresight.That same thing was very apparent here: these boys were unable to see beyond the immediate impact and worst possible outcomes of their arrest, to the bigger picture of their lives. Further down the line, Edward would no doubt have been able to find many other work opportunities and chances to travel. Joe's parents might have been initially disappointed at his decision to drive home from a party with alcohol in his system, but they were very clear they would have been there to help him back on track. Neither boy should have seen it as the end of the world. But with no one knowing what they had gone through, they only had their own thoughts to dwell on.

These cases, and others, opened up a whole conversation around how fatalistic children of that age can be, and that the guidance of an adult to broaden the spectrum and help them see beyond that mistake, is crucial. They show how a young person clearly still needs the support of an adult during and after an arrest, and that keeping a parent or guardian in the loop is the best way to ensure a young person's welfare.

We have a department in JfKL that specifically looks at strategic litigation, i.e. bringing a case to court with the main aim of helping to create wider societal change. If one of my clients has a legal issue that fits into this idea of tackling the broader picture, then I will pass the case on to them, suggesting we need to do a judicial review. Once we are in agreement, it becomes a public law case and falls under that team's remit to deal with. I effectively feed into them what happens on the ground, and they take on the roles such as instructing counsel and getting advice from barristers on the evidence – it is a true cross-JfKL team effort.

Over the years they have made some real inroads in improving the law for individuals, and also for entire groups, but the area where their work has really stood out, was in dealing with this situation with seventeen-year-olds under arrest.

In April 2013 we headed to the High Court in London, along with Hughes, his mum, and other families involved in the campaign, to hear the judgement. After hearing all the evidence and taking time to evaluate it, Lord Justice Moses ruled that it was unlawful for the police to treat seventeen-year-olds in custody the same as adults. He said it was

> ... difficult to imagine a more striking case
> where the rights of both child and parent
> under Article 8 [of the European convention
> on human rights, guaranteeing family life] are
> engaged than when a child is in custody on
> suspicion of committing a serious offence and
> needs help from someone with whom he is
> familiar and whom he trusts in redressing the
> imbalance between child and authority.

Standing and hearing the judgement with Shauneen, brave Hughes who had been prepared to push forward with this fight on behalf of others, and the parents and family members of young people who have died after being in custody, was a really exhilarating moment. Speaking to the press afterwards, Hughes summed it up: 'I didn't know my rights, whether the police were acting lawfully or unlawfully. I just needed an adult I trusted to advise me so I would have help with what I was doing.'

His mum said she felt he had been broken by the arrest at the time, and as though she had failed him, even though she hadn't been informed of what was happening. But that day when the judgement came through she was so, so proud of him – as we all were.

The Home Secretary accepted the court findings, and an appropriate adult now has to be informed when a seventeen-year-old is in custody, and present in an interview with any child up to the age of eighteen.

It was an incredible feeling for the JfKL team when the statute was changed. As a lawyer, you spend so much of your time reading legislation. So when it was amended off the back of the review, to sit and see, in black and white, the outcome of the battle we had fought, was the best feeling. There is nothing like knowing you have changed the law! It was also helpful for the charity's profile, as it received lots of coverage and was seen as a much needed change by other legal professionals too. I think we have built up a good reputation among our peers over the years anyhow, and are seen as people who really challenge the state on behalf of children, but this strategic change that helps both young people and lawyers was a powerful demonstration of it. It was a massive achievement, and an absolute high point for the charity, and one we will always be very proud of.

The change in the law has since been closely followed by the police, and every single time I represent a seventeen year old at a station and they have an appropriate adult with them, I smile to myself, and think 'we did that'.

As always, of course, that's not the end of the story when it comes to our work ensuring that seventeen-year-olds have access to the same rights as other children in the criminal justice system.

Kesia Leatherbrow was a vulnerable seventeen-year-old, who died by suicide after being arrested and held in a police cell for three days. She had broken a window trying to visit a friend, and been found in possession of a small amount of cannabis. Had she been sixteen or under, she would have been transferred to local authority care or accommodation suitable for children before she went to court on the Monday morning, but at the time a loophole in the law meant this wasn't the case. As a result, the fight for further rights for seventeen-year-olds in custody continued, and the law was eventually updated to ensure that everyone under eighteen was afforded the same treatment – now they are all regarded as the children they are.

There are still two areas we are currently looking at. Firstly, we are researching the situation for those children who turn eighteen during an ongoing criminal case – the crime was committed by a child, so should it not be dealt with as though they are still a child? This is particularly relevant in cases where the only reason they have reached adulthood before sentencing is down to incompetency by the CPS, or delays in the court system that are beyond anyone's control, such as the fall-out from the pandemic.

Child Spies

Another of our big current campaigns is challenging the Home Office in court over its use of children as spies. There is no minimum age at which a child can be used as a covert intelligence source. We were very concerned about this practice generally and yet again we found sixteen- and seventeen-year-olds were provided with fewer safeguards than younger children – which again includes access to appropriate adults – when they are used as covert informants by police and other agencies. Under the controversial Covert Human Intelligence

Sources (Criminal Conduct) Bill, children are allowed to commit crimes as part of undercover roles. Given that these children might be trafficked, in circumstances involving dangerous gangs, or might be in abusive sexual situations that they are trying to escape from, it seems absolutely crazy that not only is this allowed, but it is actively encouraged by a system that should instead be protecting the children.

As one news reporter put it when covering our campaign: 'It's been a long time since children were sent up chimneys to work – that has been frowned upon for many years – would it surprise you to know that while that is a no no for children, using them as spies is apparently just fine for the British government?'

We worked alongside the human rights charity JUSTICE, to endorse Amendment 32, which would prohibit giving children licence to commit crimes. Prior to this, we had already convinced the Home Office to amend the code to give greater protection to children, via a court case in 2019, which was paid for through crowdfunding. The case was due to be heard in the Court of Appeal, but was withdrawn in light of the changes proposed by the Home Office in 2020. The Home Office overhauled its Code of Practice to make clear that children should only be used in exceptional circumstances. We still felt it didn't go far enough though, and left the door open for children to be abused and exploited as spies, and that better safeguards needed to be put into place to protect the children's welfare and interests. In 2021, we supported Members of Parliament during the debates on the proposed amendment to the Covert Human Intelligence Sources (Criminal Conduct) Bill, that amendment was passed eventually and is now part of the Bill.

CHAPTER 11

Crown Court

While many cases involving children and young people end up in the youth court, the more serious ones are referred on to Crown Court, which is a very different world altogether.

Crown Court tends to be much more formal, with a greater emphasis on tradition and ceremony. The gowns and wigs that many people associate with court, that are absent in youth court, are often out in their full (and intimidating) glory. It is also much more of a performance, with barristers often showcasing their public-speaking talents, and judges who can be real characters. I actually spend the majority of my time in Crown Courts these days, as I am focusing on this area, and another staff member is focused on the majority of youth court cases. I prefer it in some ways, in that I feel there is more chance of sensible decisions being made in the Crown Court. A senior crown prosecutor will have reviewed the cases, barristers are more open about speaking counsel-to-counsel about the case, and there is a sense that the judges have seen it all and are generally more reasonable – not that there aren't those who have built a reputation and enjoy it; showboating by both judges and barristers is not a rarity.

Judge and Jury

One of the biggest differences in Crown Court is the fact that the decision on whether the defendant is guilty or not is made by a jury, instead of three magistrates. The jury is made up of twelve members of the public, randomly selected from the electoral roll, who sit in a couple of rows to the side of the judge. They are on chairs with small desks at which they can view any relevant documents, or in some courts now they are introducing iPads with documents previously uploaded on them. The jurors listen to all the proceedings, then go off to a private room and debate what they have seen, with the hope of coming to a unanimous decision or, if that can't be achieved, then an agreement by a majority of ten is sometimes permissible. They come back to court with their conclusion, guilty or not guilty, on each of the charges. If they can't agree, it is a 'hung jury', and it is up to the CPS to decide whether they want to run the trial all over again with a new jury.

The jurors are given quite bit of direction by the judge, especially in terms of legal matters, and the judge will also sum up the case and key evidence for them. But ultimately it is they who, off in the privacy of the jury room, decide if they have been adequately convinced of the defendant's guilt. There will always be much debate about whether the jury system is the most effective method, if it is fair or flawed, outdated or still relevant, but on the whole, I am in favour of it. It feels like society is being more involved in how they want their communities to be, as opposed to justice being an abstract notion, dealt with from afar.

I notice quite a difference though, from court to court, in the make-up of the jury and that can have quite an impact on the trial. For example, the juries at the Old Bailey are pulled from people who live within central London, which means you get a very diverse mix in all aspects – race, class, background, wealth, career, etc. – and it leads to people feeding in thoughts from all sorts of different lived experiences and expectations, and on the whole creates quite an open-minded and wide-thinking jury.

Go to a court in a more obviously affluent area of London, or a rural market town, and it can be harder for these jurors to think outside the bubble of their own experiences. The set of circumstances we are asking them to put themselves, in when thinking about a young person's actions, can be too alien for them, making it almost impossible for them to comprehend how or why a person might react in a certain way. For whatever reason, they are also more inclined to resort to thinking: 'Well, there's no smoke without fire'. There is often less sympathy or empathy for the defendant in these areas, so I'll brace myself when off for trial there – although of course, inversely, if you are a prosecutor, these are often your dream juries.

Generally speaking, though, if given a choice, I'd opt for a trial with a jury for my clients as they are more likely to see things from a human perspective where a moral argument can pay off. An exception, perhaps, is particularly technically legal cases, as they can prove difficult for jurors to get to grips with. The other exception would be for criminal exploitation and modern slavery cases, as it feels like juries still struggle with the concept, and are likely to convict as criminals people who some would see as victims of modern slavery.

The test that is put to jurors in these cases is:

A. Do you think these things happened as a result of modern slavery?

B. Do you think a reasonable person with the same
    characteristics would have felt compelled to do the
    same thing?

Nine times out of ten, the way they answer this tends to be
'Yes' to the first point, then 'No' to the second. It feels like this
is because putting themselves into the mind of someone who
has been groomed is problematic; people really struggle with
the idea unless they have experienced something a bit like it
themselves, and they always tend to imagine that they would
walk away, and not get drawn in.

Who Are the Barristers?

In the youth court, as a solicitor, we do most of the advocacy
for our client. Crown Court, though, is a different matter
as I can't actually stand up and address the court. I can do
everything behind the scenes, but that court-facing role
falls to a barrister or a solicitor advocate, who is an expert
in advocacy and public-speaking. I will deal with the client,
from the police station right through to the sentencing;
I will provide initial instructions to the barrister on the
main points around the case; then throughout the case I
will maintain contact with the client, prepare them for trial,
instruct experts, and deal with any other matters pertaining
to the preparation of their defence. The barrister will write
and present the arguments for anything that revolves around
legality and technicality of rules of evidence – for example, if
we thought there had been an abuse of process. The barrister

then addresses the court, questions the witnesses, and prepares and presents a closing speech.

Not being able to speak up can be frustrating at times, especially if I have had a change of barrister at the last minute and I don't feel they know the case as deeply as I do. It is particularly noticeable at sentencing if the barrister hasn't been involved before, and I do occasionally watch and think, 'I could have done a much better job!' But unless I take what is called the 'right of audience' exam (something I may do when my boys are older), that is how it will be for now.

As a barrister, there is a massive focus on advocacy, and areas such as writing skeleton arguments and debating at trial. But for solicitors it is much more about client care, ethics, professional conduct and day-to-day legal aid. I chose the latter route as I like to see things through from start to finish, to go on the full journey with the client and have a relationship with them. From helping make the police station experience manageable for children who are really scared about what is happening, through any charges, helping them handle court proceedings, to the acquittal or conviction, it is about the impact of it all. I couldn't just dip in and out. On the other hand, a barrister might be on one case, then be pulled off for another, and have to get their heads into cases part way through with hours to go. They are often focused on the win as opposed to the individual client, which isn't a criticism, it's the way our system is set up, so that they have to triple book themselves just to be sure of making money.

The dynamic between solicitors and barristers is generally good, but there are occasions when there might be a slight snobbishness from a barrister, implying that a solicitor is not clever enough to make the legal arguments that barristers do. But, at the end of the day, we have all done our training

– a degree, a year at Law School, then for barristers the bar vocational course, for solicitors two years as a trainee – and they are just different courses with a different focus.

Ultimately we work with some great barristers, who share the responsibility of the case with me, and establish meaningful relationships with the clients. I get to choose who I want to instruct (assuming they are also keen to be involved and are free), and I work closely with several barristers.

If we are in Crown Court for a murder trial, the case is generally led by a King's Counsel, or KC (when Queen Elizabeth II was on the throne, they were of course called Queen's Counsel.) This is the most esteemed level of barrister, and is someone who has done their time in the profession, applied to step up and been approved by a panel. The idea is they take on more technically difficult legal cases than 'normal' barristers, which inevitably means a lot of murder cases. Day in, day out, being involved in those trials must be mentally draining, but the KCs we work with do a great job. They will generally also have a supporting barrister (a junior), who they direct to take on certain roles such as cross-examining particular witnesses, generally the easier ones to give them the practice.

A barrister traditionally wears a white shirt and dark suit with a black gown over the top, and a white collar with bands, plus a short, white, horsehair wig. Once promoted to KC, the gown is of a different cut, and was traditionally silk – hence the term sometimes used for becoming a KC: 'taking silk'. As a solicitor, the clothing isn't as traditional – I wear dark-coloured formal wear, so generally a black, blue or grey suit, trousers, dress, or skirt. The judge will also traditionally wear a gown and wig, although less formal wear is often seen as more appropriate when dealing with children.

Adjustments for Children

The guidance for a trial involving a young person in Crown Court is that reasonable adjustments should be made to the process to help them actually engage with what is happening, to understand what is being said and the decisions that are being made, and to reduce the intimidating atmosphere wherever possible. But until recently the guidance was very rarely put into practice.

JfKL became involved in an appeal case for a murder conviction on joint enterprise. We lost the appeal, but many of the arguments we put forward were about the lack of adjustments made for the two defendants by the court. Throughout the trial they sat in the dock next to each other, not engaging in their trial at all but just messing about. Instead of the legal professionals adjusting the language used so the boys could understand it, or the judge moving them next to their lawyers, as per the practice direction, the boys were just berated for their behaviour.

As a result of that appeal case, however, now Crown Courts have to actually follow the practice directions, or if not, actively state why they are not doing so. The onus is now meant to be on them to take steps such as removing wigs and gowns, allowing children to sit out of the dock, near or with their lawyers, giving adequate breaks, making adjustments to the language used, or having an appropriate adult with the young people to ensure they understand what is happening.

So, thankfully, the comments in this case have led to quite a change, although I've found that it does still rely on the judge believing in that way of working and managing it, or a lawyer who is willing to challenge the lack of adjustments. Recently I represented a boy who had just turned eighteen, alongside a group of those who were under eighteen. Because of my client's age I couldn't make any arguments to the court for adjustments, and none of the other lawyers did, so it continued in the usual vein. While this might be 'just another murder case' to them, for this young person it is probably the scariest, most intimidating thing they have ever dealt with, and it's not good enough to have them sitting there overwhelmed, left in the dark about their future. There is still a degree to which the legal profession is so used to processing children through the system, that they don't overly think about it. That, along with the whole element of tradition, leads some people to see it as an affront to the profession to say 'let's remove the traditional garb'.

On the whole, I don't think lawyers challenge the judges and the court enough. They adopt a subservient and accepting attitude, not questioning or fighting the client's corner hard enough, particularly when it relates to issues around pomp and ceremony. I understand that the system works on having respect for the judge, and it takes a bit of bravery as a lawyer to say, 'That isn't appropriate for these young people', but I see it as a crucial part of our job to flag up when that is the case. Of course, I don't want to annoy the judge, so there is a way to make these challenges respectfully, but if by doing my job I do annoy them, then so be it – I'd rather take that over avoiding conflict and letting my client down. Thankfully a lot of the barristers we work with are equally keen to push the young person's side, and will also take these risks.

The UK's Adversarial System

The legal systems in use across the UK, Europe and the US tend to fall into two categories: adversarial and inquisitorial systems. It is good to be aware of both and consider the different methods.

Inquisitorial systems see the judge do exactly that – inquire into the case in order to try to get to the truth. The judge can ask the lawyers about any area they wish to, and get them to call any witness they wish to hear from. The idea is to search out evidence that will help give a clear picture of what has happened. The focus is on finding out the truth. If the judge feels in the end that the search shows there is a case against the defendant, then it goes to trial. This system is used across most of Europe and definitely has its advantages, but also has its flaws.

The adversarial system used in the UK and America sees the prosecution and the defence set up as adversaries, battling it out to convince the judge and jury that their side is to be believed. They can choose which issues to focus on, what evidence is produced, and who they call to be witnesses. The judge is there very much to oversee what is happening, controlling everything about how the trial is run, from how long we sit in court and when the breaks are, to what evidence can be admitted, and what it is appropriate for the jury to hear and see. The style of the judge is more as a font of knowledge on the law, clarifying any issues and making sure the correct procedure is followed. He also sums up the facts at the end, before the jury goes out to deliberate whose side they will come down on. The focus in this system is on whether someone is guilty or innocent, and if found guilty you are then only left with the possibility of appealing after conviction.

Like all systems, there are pros and cons, but in UK courts at times it can almost feel like a theatre, where everyone has their role to play, and accepts what everyone else is doing and the way they have to act. So there is a very specific role for the prosecution, then the defence must act in a certain way, while the judge is there as a kind of overlord, keeping the whole court process going.

There are rules on every aspect, such as how you have to approach a witness in order to challenge the evidence on behalf of a client, and there is so much protocol in place to keep the wheels turning and the whole case moving forward. It is certainly less theatrical in the UK than the American courts, but there are times when it feels like a battle between who has the better lawyer on their side, rather than whether the defendant is guilty or innocent.

The Old Bailey

Ask anyone to name a court in the UK, and inevitably their mind will turn to the Old Bailey, also known as the Central Criminal Court of England and Wales. Established in the sixteenth century, it is an institution steeped in history, and has become the best-known criminal court in the world. Any major criminal case from within Greater London and the surrounding areas has a high chance of being heard there. An engraved plaque over the main entrance says: 'Defend the Children of the Poor, and Punish the Wrongdoer.' It is a quote from the Bible, Psalm 72, and always strikes me as ironic as, more often than not, it feels like it is the poorer children that we are prosecuting. Going down into the cells it can feel like a sea of poor, young – mainly black – boys, waiting to be booked in, one after the other.

We don't do many murder cases at JfKL – our aim is to support our young clients in difficult situations before things have become even remotely close to that being a scenario. But lots of firms literally survive by taking on one murder case after another, and inevitably this means that they often fall into a formulaic way of doing things. It can be incredibly depressing.

Visitors come from all over to watch one of the Old Bailey trials, and there are tours of the undeniably impressive building. However, when it comes to cases involving children, I don't think it is the best place. The very aspects that make it fascinating to visitors often make it inappropriate to young defendants. The court's layout has tradition and formality at its heart, leaving it feeling antiquated and intimidating to most adults facing trial there, let alone children and young people. The judge sits up in a high dock, the lawyers in the well of the court, with the young people in a glass dock behind them. Members of the public are up in the high gallery, looking down on proceedings, meaning family and friends of the prosecution and defence are often all sitting there side by side. Unsurprisingly, this increases anger and tension, and comments are inevitably exchanged between the two groups.

The exception to the gallery rule is close family members of the deceased in a murder trial, who are allowed down into the court. This can be quite intimidating as a defence lawyer, as doing my job and advancing the position for the defence means I can be at the receiving end of passive-aggressive comments and resentful looks. But at the end of the day, in the family's mind I am representing the person or people who might have been involved in the death of their child.

It is not just the court layout and outfits that seem dated: many of the traditions and ways things are done represent a bizarre nod to the past, that actually have no place in the present, but regardless, everyone just goes along with them. One of those that irritated me on a personal level when I was first working in law is the Advocates Mess, a kind of dining room/quiet area, available for barristers to base themselves in to get on with their work. As a solicitor I want to be discussing case strategy or reflecting on evidence with my team, the junior barrister and King's Counsel, but in theory I was not qualified to be in the Mess. I tended to ignore the rule though, and no one complained that I shouldn't be there, and over time, thankfully, it seems to have opened its doors more widely. Equally, the pictures of the inspirational legal figures are dominated by old white men, but I believe there is talk that these will be updated soon. The robing rooms are the next things that need to be addressed – women have a much smaller robing room than men, reflective of past expectations that it was a male profession.

I don't know if, deep down, most lawyers disagree with traditions and rules such as these, or whether they have just become inured to them. I wonder if, for many barristers, as they have worked and fought so hard to pass the bar, to call out anything that it represents as ridiculous might feel as if it undermines their achievement, so they just pretend it is fine. Criminal law can feel like a closed shop at times – once you're in, and see that all the goods inside aren't quite as great as you imagined, you just have to keep quiet about it.

Teenage Witnesses

What happens if a child ends up in the legal system through an event or action that doesn't involve them as the defendant, but because they are a witness?

Let's take a step back from court, and look at the witness experience from the moment of the police involvement. It might be that police attended at the time of the incident and took the names and details of witnesses, perhaps names were passed to them at a later date, or perhaps they tracked the young person down, for example using CCTV. But whatever the case, a child is now being talked to by police as a potential witness. This is the one situation at the police station where I would say a lawyer isn't necessary. Assuming the child genuinely wasn't involved in any way, and isn't about to incriminate themselves, talking about what they have seen or experienced should not be problematic. Compared to dealing with defendants, the police are generally much more child-orientated in their approach in this situation, and will aim to make the witness feel as comfortable as possible, for example taking a statement from the child in their own home.

One key difference in an interview with a child witness versus an adult, is that the police need to make sure that the child actually understands the difference between the truth and a lie. This might sound very basic, but it is extraordinary how often the line is quite blurred in a child's mind. Sometimes children make allegations that simply aren't true, out of fear, an inability to see the bigger picture, or out of a genuine lack of understanding of what it is to be honest. So the Truth and Lies Discussion test has to be carried out on tape as part of the recorded interview, with the child told that: 'We are seeking to achieve your best evidence, and it is important that you understand what is truth, and what is lies'.

As I said before in Chapter 8, for this test the officer will give a simple example and ask the child to confirm whether it is a truth or lie.

From this point, the witness is now theoretically under the care of the Crown Prosecution Service (CPS), although apart from receiving information on when they are due in court from the witness service or police liaison officer, a lot of the time the witness doesn't know what is happening until they turn up to trial. That is generally when they meet the lawyer for the first time, and have a chat about what they might be asked (this might only differ for a particularly high profile or serious trial). People imagine they will be given a practice run-through, and when this doesn't happen, we are often contacted at JfKL and asked if we can represent them as a prosecution witness. Unfortunately we have to tell them that the CPS is effectively their lawyer and that they need to contact them if they have any questions.

It is a completely different scenario with our specific defence witnesses. We meet them in advance and take their statements, know what they will say in advance of the day, and keep in touch with them about court dates, make sure they can get there, etc. We are not allowed to coach them, but they will have a clear idea of all the evidence in the case, when and why they are coming to court, and what they can expect. It is intimidating for anyone to give evidence, let alone a child, so we always want to give them as much support as possible.

People ask if they are obliged to appear as a witness, and the answer is that if the police have your details, and they feel it is in the interest of justice for the court to hear your evidence, then it is hard to avoid. A person can be summoned to court, which is a court notice requiring a person to attend the hearing. If they choose to ignore the notice and are not responding to police contact, in some cases the police will pick that person up and bring them to court. It is not ideal, as there is a risk that the person will become a hostile witness and refuse to say anything, or even provide a completely different account. The best advice I can give someone who has been asked to be a witness but doesn't want to be, is to make their position clear to the officer in the case, the witness service and the CPS as soon as possible and continue to do so in the run-up to the trial. I can understand why it is not for everyone. Giving evidence in a serious trial might mean putting yourself at risk.

As a side note, a witness protection programme does exist in the UK, managed by the UK Protected Persons Service (UKPPS), but thanks to the significant amount of money involved and the level of sign-off they need, it is extremely unlikely to be offered to witnesses in all but the most extreme cases. It is a complete fantasy to imagine that your average person, even in a serious murder case, is going to be offered a place on a witness protection programme.

Sometimes the court has to accept that a person might have originally given a witness statement, but they just are not prepared to stand up in court, and have perhaps changed their mind about proceeding at all. This often arises when a case involves family relationships, and the court can see that giving evidence may well cause that person more problems in the long-term. For example, if they had witnessed violence involving a family member, they might later want to retract this, and the best a prosecutor can then do is apply for their witness statement to be read or played (if video recorded) as hearsay evidence. However, we will often challenge that, because as defence lawyers we want to be able to cross-examine that witness in person. If a judge agrees with us, he will tell the prosecution they either have to proceed without the witness, or drop the case.

There are a number of rights currently in place for witnesses, which aim to make their time in court as painless as possible. These include the right to ask to give evidence via video from another room, or behind a screen. These special measures are available for any witness who believes that the quality of their evidence will be improved by the measure being in place. While these are routinely asked for for prosecution witnesses, it is rare for lawyers to flag these rights to children who are defendants in criminal proceedings. But they absolutely can ask for special measures, backing up their requests with the relevant supporting assessments, such as from a psychologist or speech and language therapist, so it is good to be aware that this is an option.

One of the biggest issues for me with young prosecution witnesses, though, is the fact that they are only there to serve the bigger picture of the case at hand, but very little thought is given to their own well-being, or the impact of the incident on them. Unless they are the victim at the centre of the trial, it is extremely unlikely that they will be offered any support, despite potentially having witnessed something incredibly traumatic and life-changing.

One particular set of witnesses always stands out in my mind as being let down on this front – and, in fact, let down across the board as young people. They were appearing at the trial of three teens accused of murdering another teen. From their evidence it was clear they had been failed by the multiple public services that exist to protect them. It felt as if no one was getting anything right for them, and they had already been written off by society. They could have been there as witnesses or defendants that day: the cards the two groups had been dealt weren't any different.

The incident had happened on a school day, and most of the witnesses explained that they were not currently attending mainstream education. It felt as though they hadn't been prepared for the court process, and were scared and out of their depth. Some of them were really hostile from the second they were on the stand, and it was clear from the way they spoke that their previous experiences with the police and the law had not been positive. All of the witnesses were between fourteen and sixteen years old and showing clear signs of trauma – almost inevitable when they had not only seen a boy die, but he was their peer – and their statements all made it clear their mental health had been affected. Yet their emotions and well-being before giving evidence clearly hadn't been addressed. There were a lot of issues around guilt about what they should or shouldn't have done that day: some had run away from the scene and were now questioning if they could have saved their friend had they stayed; equally, there was the realization that it could just as easily have been them who could have been killed.

One girl seemed like she had pulled down all the shutters on her life. She spoke about having sex on her thirteenth birthday, without batting an eyelid. You could see the trauma in her eyes as she continued to speak; it was just so awful.

But sadly, as witnesses for the prosecution, the support they would have been offered is minimal. Everyone is focused on getting through the trial and prosecuting the accused. They just want the witnesses to turn up and give evidence, but little thought is given to the well-being of these scared children who are hardening their minds to the world by the minute, just in order to survive.

It felt so bleak, so depressing, my heart broke a little for each of them that day, and I felt that this wasn't the end of it: this case was going to have a ripple effect for years to come.

How could we really expect them to just walk away from that court, and get on with their lives?

Sure enough, as I continue to work in the local area, over the next year I saw the names of several of those witnesses popping up in court cases – but no longer as a witness, this time as the accused. I haven't represented any of them, because the previous court connection means I am not allowed to, but I am aware of what is happening to them. The failings are continuing. The devastation from that one death is having much wider consequences. There needs to be a long, hard look at the bigger picture, and real, tangible improvements to our handling of child witnesses. We need an approach that puts their welfare front and foremost in the lead-up to the trial, during it, and, if needed, in the months beyond.

How Much Does a Lawyer Cost?

Naturally one of the first questions that comes to mind for many parents when thinking of getting a lawyer involved in a situation with their child, is: 'How much will it cost me? Can I afford it?'

The general rule of thumb in UK law is that everyone, adult or child, is entitled to free legal advice at the police station, regardless of age or the crime. Whether an adult receives legal aid beyond that, to cover the cost of a lawyer in any further proceedings in court or otherwise, is based on your means. If you earn over approximately £200 a week you will not be eligible for legal aid in the magistrates' court and will need to represent yourself. Under that figure, and you are entitled to legal aid. In the Crown Court things work slightly differently and most people are granted legal aid, but if you earn over a certain amount you will be expected to make a monthly contribution to your legal aid fees, of up to £1,000 per month.

When it comes to children, people often imagine the decision will be based on their parents' income, but that is not the case for criminal legal aid – thankfully any child under under eighteen will be granted legal aid if it is in the interest of justice for that child to be represented. This is the case in pretty much all criminal justice circumstances for young people, with very rare exceptions. Occasionally, a child who has been charged with possession of cannabis or a driving offence might be refused it. The legal aid team might see it as a straightforward case, and the magistrates will ask them the necessary questions without the need for a lawyer. But again, I will always challenge that. You can't expect a child to represent themselves in court, no matter what the circumstances. You need a lawyer to go behind the formalities, explain to the client what will happen, their options, how they will be connected with the Youth Offending Team and what to expect from the process.

Besides, a thirteen-year-old being convicted of smoking cannabis or shoplifting may seem like a small issue to the CPS, but it can be a huge issue to the child, and have a significant impact on their future. At this stage, there is still so much that can be done to support children and young people, which is one of the main reasons I chose to dedicate my career to cases involving them, rather than adults. I am fuelled by hope – and there is so much more hope in working with children and young people. They are still at a stage where an event or interaction with the right person can change the course of their situation and effectively their life. It is too easy to write off the 'naughty kid', but I try to be that person who can work out why they keep getting caught up in the legal system, understand what is going on, listen to their perspective and try to help source the things they might need to help them. And that is why I would argue that they should ALWAYS be represented.

It is also why at JfKL we see taking on legal representation of a child as more than just knowing the law and reeling off the best arguments. We are as much counsellors and confidants as legal representation. In order to be successful, you have to be able to quickly gain the trust of a young person, and that can be very tough. Unless you have been recommended to them through a friend or, say, they know you are a trusted individual at their local youth club, they generally see you as just another part of the system, which is really unfortunate. It is particularly hard for those who are acting as a duty solicitor at the police station because, as much as lawyers will try to explain their role, the young person will see it as this person has been appointed to their case by the police, and is therefore 'one of them'.

The relationship between a solicitor and their client is protected by what is called legal privilege. This means that all written or spoken communication between a client and their lawyer is privileged, and cannot be disclosed as part of the legal proceedings or otherwise. For a lot of children it will be the first time they have been told, 'You are in charge of this relationship, you instruct me. As your lawyer, anything you tell me I can't tell anyone without your permission. I can't do anything about your case that you tell me not to.'

Once they have accepted that, for a lot of young people it can be an opportunity to get some things off their chest, because they feel in control of what happens with that information, and then that trust can allow you to get to the bottom of what is going on and how best you can help them change their current circumstances. For most of the children and young people we represent, achieving the right outcome at the right time can change the trajectory of their life. Not only does it mean they do not need to go through life explaining a conviction but, more importantly, they don't start adult life feeling hopeless. The weight of being considered an 'offender' is for some young people just too much to bear and becomes part of their identity: they feel as if they are barred from being anything else. The labels we give young people begin to define them.

As a side note here, while I am a strong believer in this being the right way round – that the client is in charge of their relationship and has the ability to make their own decisions – occasionally it can prove frustrating. This is because we can advise, but we can't make decisions that go against our client's wishes, no matter whether we deem it in their best interest or not. The court system has to acknowledge something called the Welfare Principle, which means it is meant to focus on the best interest of the child, but as the child's lawyer, you have to respond to their instructions, not their best interest. This can be quite difficult to convey to a child, as every adult in their life is normally there to act in their best interest, to make decisions about them that they might not always agree with. But not in our case.

This can be particularly hard when, for example, I can see a direction that would be the right one for the child, but it's a direction they are choosing not to go with.

This is common when the child has co-defendants in the dock with them, which can prove to be a minefield. The child will often say they don't want to advance a position that might damage their peers, or they might have to admit to something such as learning difficulties that they don't want others to know about. It is also a common scenario in exploitation cases, in which the child might have told you something, but they are absolutely adamant that they don't want it repeated outside of our meeting.

To know I have had cases where the outcome could have been different had I been able to decide the defence, is heartbreaking. I watched a girl go to prison for two years for hiding a firearm in her bedroom that was given to her by her boyfriend, as she would never let me suggest she had been groomed. She was sixteen when the weapon was discovered. He was seven years older, a known criminal in the area, and the police were watching him at the time. If she had cooperated with them, and been honest about the situation, she could have walked free, but she wanted to protect him. Everyone in that courtroom could clearly see that she had been groomed, but she wouldn't let me make the relevant legal arguments, so a custodial sentence was the judge's only option. Unsurprisingly, she is no longer with that man, but we have kept in touch (as I do with many of my clients), and she is getting on with her life: it's just a real shame that she spent that time in prison unnecessarily.

Ultimately, that idea of not disclosing any information without a client's permission is paramount, and one of our ethical duties as a lawyer. The only time you can breach it is to stop a crime happening, or to prevent someone from being caused serious harm. I do try to be quite innovative though, and occasionally will ask my client if they will agree to me getting the Youth Offending Team (YOT) to explore a certain area with them further. A YOT's duty of confidentiality is entirely different from mine as the defence solicitor, so if the client opens up to them, it may be that the issue can become evidence in court. I'll always be clear that is the case, but it is just one way in which I am doing my best to consider the client's welfare, as well as the law.

At the police station it is tough, as it is left in the hands of the child and the parent as to whether they take on a lawyer. A child might say they don't want one, without really understanding why they would need one, and the parent might override that and say, 'I don't care what they say, they have to wait for a lawyer.' But others will just feel out of their depth, worried that it might cost, and think the quicker it is over and done with the better. So their child goes into the interview unrepresented, without a clue as to how to navigate the system, and actually the process can take much longer, and lead to a higher chance of prosecution.

For purposes of transparency, let's talk about what a lawyer gets from legal aid. If arrested, in the police station everyone is entitled to free legal representation, whether adult or child. It is only later, if heading to court, that the means tests are added in. So, lawyers are paid a fixed fee of approximately £220 (the rates vary across the country) for everything at the police station, whether the person has been arrested for shoplifting or murder.

This means talking with and prepping the client before they go into the police interview, then sitting in with them. The absolute shortest time this would be, is around sixty to ninety minutes of the solicitor's time, but in the majority of cases it is much longer.

The only time you get paid more than this is if you do enough hours to fall into the exceptional fee system, but realistically that never happens. I would have to be in consultation and interview with the client for around twelve hours, which is difficult to justify in most circumstances, unless there are multiple interviews. But then there is the time chasing up with the police afterwards, letters and phone calls to the client, the overheads for the firm … it isn't very long before you are working at a loss. For that reason, many law firms will only do the initial work at the station for the fee – i.e. the bare minimum. They will deal with the interview, then that's it; there is a cap on what they will do without further payment. The problem is that a lot of the time with children, if you want to make sure everything possible is done to see that they aren't prosecuted, you might have to follow up with written representations to the police or the CPS. Unless it is clear there is no evidence, I will spend time researching and looking up arguments and reasons why it is not in the public interest to prosecute. It requires lots of time and effort, and therefore entails work well beyond the fee.

Then there are the fees a lawyer gets for appearing in court. There is a fixed fee system in place at magistrates' courts, so for a guilty plea, the lawyer will get less than £300. If it goes to trial, there is another fixed fee bracket.

In Crown Court you are not paid on how much work you do, but bizarrely by the number of pages of prosecution evidence. This is particularly problematic for certain types of cases – for example rape or sexual assault, when there might only be two people present, the victim and the defendant, so pages of evidence and interview transcripts may be minimal. But obviously if someone is charged with rape this can be life-changing for both sides, so to prepare for that case is a huge amount of work, and to do right by your client you really need to put those hours in. But you are being paid very little for it. Every now and then you will get a case with lots of paper evidence, for example a lot of telephone records – and frankly we need a few of those types of cases every year just to help us with funds for the rest of the cases.

In days gone by there might have been a time when the criminal legal system was a profitable profession to enter, but now ... I would dispute that, hence why solicitors and barristers are leaving the profession in droves. I know people are always dubious about that, as the perception of 'fat cat lawyers' has persisted, but it certainly doesn't apply to criminal law. Even as I am writing this, barristers have been striking over pay issues, so you really can only go into this profession for the love of the job, and the difference you hope to make to people's lives. If money is your drive, you are in for a big shock!

JfKL is a registered charity and as such we are very lucky to get grants and funding. But the problem is that those tend to be more directed towards our additional work such as youth projects and our non-legal advocacy, such as sending youth advocates along to meetings with social workers to make sure their voices are heard, or constructive conclusions are reached. We also do reasonably well with grants towards our legal work with housing and trying to house homeless young people, and when we take strategic cases to challenge the law for all children, funders are generally relatively good at helping out.

When it comes to individual criminal proceedings though, the day-to-day cases, it is a different matter. The perception is that legal aid should be covering this, so it is much tougher to get the extra money needed to tide us over in that area. People aren't interested in helping towards something they think should be covered by the courts. The reality is that with the little bits of grants we can get towards it, and the legal aid income, we just about cover costs for criminal cases. But as I hope you have seen throughout the book so far, what happens in the police station and in court for a young person entering the legal system can be so crucial to their future, as well as having a ripple effect on so many around them. Society as a whole will benefit if those young people have proper representation and support, and funding is paramount to ensuring that happens.

CHAPTER 12

Different Sentencing Options

Ask people what kind of punishments someone might face for a crime, and they are sure to instantly think of prison or, for a lesser offence, maybe community service or a fine. In reality there are numerous different options available to both the police and judges when concluding a case, many of which are considered for the more minor crimes long before a custodial sentence comes into play. They may even be settled on without the person who has been charged having to go to court. If our clients accept they have committed a crime, or are found guilty, it will always be our aim to seek a non-custodial sentence, and ideally have the matter dealt with without them even having to set foot in a courtroom.

The lowest outcome or 'disposal' that can be given to a young person is a community resolution. The courts aren't involved in this and it doesn't appear on the client's criminal record. It is a matter between the police and the child or young person, and sees them signing a basic agreement about their future behaviour. It might say something as simple as they will refrain from using cannabis, or if they have been caught committing very minor criminal damage such as breaking a neighbour's window with a football, it could be that their parents will pay the cost of having it repaired. Occasionally there is a choice in some of these situations for any victim of the crime to have some input too, and the matter is often dealt with quite quickly.

The next level up from this includes a whole raft of what are called out-of-court disposals, such as youth cautions and youth conditional cautions. When handed one of these the child still doesn't have to attend court, but the conviction will appear on a criminal record. They are, however, considered 'spent' as soon as they are given, which means that while the conviction might have to be disclosed in certain circumstances (for example, as part of any future criminal proceedings), they don't have to be declared on job applications, and they don't appear on DBS checks (the Disclosure and Barring Service checks that flag criminal convictions). These out-of-court disposals are given out by the police, often in conjunction with the YOT, who will pull together a programme or package for the young person with the idea of giving them some extra guidance, and minimizing future offending.

If it is felt necessary that the young person goes to court, but it is the first time they have been in trouble and they plead guilty from the start, it is possible they will be given a Referral Order. Again, this appears on a criminal record, but means that instead of going through the formality of the legal system, they will be referred to a panel made up of two volunteers from the local community and a YOT officer. This trio will sit down with the child and their parents or guardians, and come up with a contract of behaviour that needs to be adhered to for up to a year. The idea is that this is monitored throughout the agreed time period, and at the end there is a review meeting at which, if the panel decides the contract has been followed successfully, the conviction is now deemed 'spent'.

Then there are Youth Rehabilitation Orders, where there might be elements of restorative justice and the young person will be required to do a certain number of reparation hours. This is quite different from the image so many people have in their minds from the past – you are less likely to see teens in a high-vis jacket, picking chewing gum off benches, or scrubbing graffiti off walls, and more likely to see them working in a youth club or charity shop. The idea is that they might get something more out of it on an educational or empathetic level, and ideally learn some life skills in the process. This restorative justice can also be part of a Referral Order or caution, and can give the victim an opportunity to meet or communicate with the young person, such as through mediation or an apology letter.

I'd like to see more of this way of dealing with crime involving young people, as I think it can be really effective. In the past there was a Restorative Justice Worker in the YOT who was responsible for reparation projects, such as gardening, or helping in the local community. They would also oversee face-to-face meetings between the young person and the victim, if both parties felt that would be beneficial to moving on from the incident. But from what I can see there is rarely a designated post for that now as there aren't enough resources going into that aspect of the legal system in the UK, which I think is a shame.

Meetings with the YOT can take all sorts of different formats, and when done right, can be highly effective. It is a great opportunity to work with young people in a way that can make a real difference to them, and to society as a whole. At times you might be focusing on practical advice, such as helping the young person find a weekend job for a source of income, or looking at educational courses they might pursue. Other times it can become more like counselling: 'What is your relationship like with your parents?', 'What makes you want to smoke cannabis?' or simply, 'What do you want to talk to me about today?'

Other times it might just be a general conversation: 'Tell me about your friendship group,' or 'What have you been doing today?' I loved my time in that role earlier in my career, as the hands-on aspect where you get to focus on the roots of the issues for the child, their outlook and experience will always be my favoured approach. I felt the role allowed me a chance to make a difference.

I would see young people on bail packages three times a week, which gave room for a genuine connection, but the downside is you are part of the enforcement process, so a young person has to attend the appointments or they get into further trouble. If they missed a meeting, the initial step was to issue a warning, then it became a final warning, and then on the third occasion the YOT officer had to return the young person to court. We used to have a system called Caseworks, where all appointments were logged and if someone didn't make it to a meeting, a message would flash up: 'Warning, order has been breached'. I would always try to help the young person make up for it in the first instance – I'd say, 'Okay, you haven't come to your appointment today, but if you make it at another point this week, I can still mark it that you have attended, and we can avoid this becoming a problem.' If there was a way to help them back on track, I'd rather that, than simply escalating the problem to someone else, and causing a setback for the young person involved. Talking to friends who work in similar roles now, they are still battling these same systems today.

Then there are custodial sentences, something I am against being handed out to children for many reasons, one being that it alienates them further from society and teaches them to survive in a way that is often detrimental to life in the outside world. The suggestion that a custodial sentence is rehabilitation rather than punishment really doesn't stack up – you only have to look at the statistics. When more than two-thirds of children reoffend within twelve months of release from secure institutions, you can hardly claim that the institutions are having the desired effect. Rates dropped in the statistics for the years 2020–21, but given the effect of Covid, courts being closed, children at home, etc., it didn't really feel like a true reflection. And, ultimately, that long-term trend of going into custody, coming out, reoffending, is a cycle that starts in teenagers, and then they are stuck in it for life. Yet another reason not to send children into custody.

When it comes to custodial sentences, there are three main types that can be handed out to young people: detention and training orders, longer custodial sentences, and life sentences. Detention and training orders last between four months and two years, and mean a young person spends half their sentence in a young offender institution, and the other half out in the community, but under supervision. There will be certain restrictions put on their lifestyle and behaviour, dependent on the crime they have committed. Longer custodial sentences are similar, but the percentage of time in custody can vary, with the time back in the community spent 'on licence'. This term means that the young person has to meet certain criteria, and that if they commit any other crime during that period they will be straight back to prison to complete their sentence.

Anyone who is found guilty of murder must be given a life sentence. The 'life' bit often causes confusion, but it is misunderstood. It doesn't mean that the offender is being jailed for life, but more that they are now within the criminal legal system for life. So when deciding on a life sentence, a judge will also determine a number of years in custody before the person is eligible for parole and then, once released, they are on licence for the rest of their life. For children the mandatory sentence for a person found guilty of murder is not life but detention at His Majesty's pleasure, and the starting point for the minimum term is twelve years. Generally, the length of the custodial sentence for a young person will be shorter than for an adult who has committed the same crime.

Obviously, there is a degree of subjectivity as to what sentence every crime deserves. There are guidelines issued by the Sentencing Council, an independent public body, and courts must follow those, unless it is in the interest of justice not to do so. But there is a fair bit of flexibility within that, and it can depend a lot on the individual magistrate or judge.

Custodial sentences are carried out by young people in one of three places:

- Young Offender Institution (YOI)

- Secure Training Centre (STC)

- Secure Children's Home (SCH)

The main differences are that YOIs are for those aged fifteen and over, and generally house hundreds of young people; STCs are for children aged twelve and over and are of a medium size; and SCHs can take those who are ten and over, and have a small number of children at a time. Decisions on which institution is appropriate are made by the Youth Offending Team liaising with the Youth Justice Board placements team.

In chapter one I made my feelings clear about YOIs and the detrimental effect they have on so many children. I am aware that there are more progressive ideas being considered at present, such as secure colleges of which, in theory, I would be more supportive. However, sadly, whatever the institution, I feel that the same problems will arise due to the systemic failure and institutional racism that is embedded in our public services. I think we need to look at much more innovative, therapeutic, community-led and community-based initiatives.

Was it Fair?

However, after years of working with young people, I can say that the biggest factor that influences how a young person feels after a court case is often not the actual outcome, or what they see as their punishment, but whether they felt that the process was fair. If they feel it was settled in an unjust manner, that more than anything is what causes the anger, upset and frustration and they lose any faith they had in the system. When the sentence doesn't seem to reflect the true nature of the crime, at best a young person can be left with a bad taste in their mouth, and at worst, a sentence and outlook that changes the course of their life.

I had a case of a sixteen-year-old boy, Paul, who was hanging out with three of his friends, and in a moment of madness they decided to break into a local football club. My client has autism and anxiety, doesn't find it that easy to make friends and, as a result, doesn't always make the best decisions – going along with this plan being one of them.

The boys jumped the fence, broke into the clubhouse and committed criminal damage on a relatively small, but still disrespectful and frustrating scale: for example, they pulled over the tub of hand sanitizer so it spilt across the floor. Then they decided to turn their attention to a school next to the football club, and started throwing stones at the windows. At this point Paul was beginning to have real doubts about what was happening, so when his friend picked up a brick to chuck at the windows he decided it was too much and ran off, leaving them to it. The rest of the boys then broke into the school, smashed up security cameras, locks, tables and art equipment. In total, the day's rampage caused just shy of £10,000 worth of damage – £942 in the football club, and the rest in the school.

When arrested, Paul immediately admitted to his part, and I looked for him to be dealt with separately to the others and get an out-of-court disposal. But the police and Youth Offending Team decided the boys all needed to be dealt with together, and because of the cost of the overall damage, decided it was something that would have to go to court. The headteacher of the school had written a statement about how horrible it had been for the reception staff and students, as the broken windows meant they had to be boarded up, changing the inside lighting, and they were scared at the idea that people had broken in. It wasn't a nice picture and anyone listening couldn't help but feel sorry for these confused four-year-olds. However, as I emphasized, my client had nothing to do with that.

In court, I argued that Paul had left before the serious damage was done, and that, as a vulnerable young person, choosing to stand up and walk away from that kind of peer pressure was a particularly big decision for him to have made. It was in some ways an achievement in his personal development.

The first question the magistrate put to my client was: 'So, what were you thinking?' It was a near impossible question for an autistic boy to answer, to recall his thought processes from an event that, thanks to the speed of the court system, was now a year ago. This was then followed up by: 'How do you feel?' Again, as you will remember from the chapter on mental health, this is often an incredibly difficult question for an autistic person to formulate a response to. I was fuming, but asked them to consider an out-of-court disposal for Paul. The magistrates refused, and instead decided to lump all the defendants together during the sentencing, giving them Referral Orders and imposing a £2,000 compensation order against each of them.

The magistrates said they wanted the school to get compensation. It wasn't necessary, as the damage was covered by insurance, but I understand they wanted the boys to realize the financial impact of their actions, as well as the loss of time and the upset caused to those who found the damage. Except, as I again tried to flag, Paul was not involved in the majority of the damage and, as none of the boys had that kind of money, it was effectively a fine for the parents.

The one concession to the fact Paul hadn't been involved in the majority of the damage was that his Referral Order was one month shorter than the rest of the boys. It seemed incredibly unjust and didn't reflect the balance of the situation between the boys.

Paul was confused by it all, and his dad was furious. He had been a pub landlord before this incident, and when Paul was arrested, the family were so worried he was going down the wrong path, his father gave up the pub in order to spend more time with his son. He set up his own catering business so he could dictate his own hours. They moved out of the area, and Paul was refocusing his life, he practised baking and set up his own business, and both physically and mentally moved on. A year later, when this finally all went to trial, things had very much changed for him – and a year is a long time in a young person's mind. You have to ask how this punishment helped the positive situation he was in by then, and when is a young person allowed to move on from their mistakes? Working on cases like that end up leaving me so disappointed.

It is important for children to understand when they have made a good decision, and that the system is going to be just and fair and take that on board. In Paul's mind it was a case of, 'I know I did wrong, I'm sorry for what I did, but then I could see it was going too far, so I made a good and difficult decision and left. I don't make friends easily, so to stand up to those I do have, was really hard, but I did it.'

For any young person it would be hard to get your head around the fact that all the aspects you did right are being ignored, but for somebody who is autistic and sees things very literally, in black and white, what sense of fairness was he going to take away from this process? If you want people to respect the legal process, it has to be fair. I get frustrated that people can't take themselves back to the mind of their fifteen-year-old selves, and the impact of peer pressure. Maybe those magistrates just thought, 'Well, I would never have gone and damaged the football club in the first place.' This was a chance for an authentic, teachable moment, and I literally spelled that out in my mitigation – the court has an important role here to send a message to the young person about the decision he made – but no, the magistrates had made up their minds. The system could be so much better if it just looked at these young people as individuals, and how they could genuinely be helped to improve in life. But opportunities like that are missed by the courts all the time.

A Friendly Neighbourhood Bobby?

At the other end of the scale, I want to mention a misplaced idea that parents sometimes have, that a policeman can just 'have a word' with their child about some misdemeanour or another. The policing system has long moved on from the days when your local bobby might give a child a cuff around the ear and send them on their way with a stern word about not helping themselves to sweets from the local shop, or your friendly neighbourhood officer might pop in for a cup of tea with a set of parents and let them know that their son's penchant for fighting was going to get him in trouble if he didn't put a stop to it. And while the idea of it feels very quaint, old England, it was only a generation or two back that we would have seen that kind of policing as normal. So, it is understandable that some people still assume this kind of corrective policing, that avoids young people getting into the actual legal system, might still exist. The reality is, it doesn't.

We've had situations in which a parent, struggling to control their child, has actually called the police, under the illusion that they will just have a chat with them and help set the child on the straight and narrow. One mum found cannabis in her son's bedroom and, keen to shock him with a lecture from the police, gave them a call. But the next minute, when her son was being carted off to the police station, the poor woman rang JfKL in a panic – only to find there was very little we could do. I had to explain that those kinds of friendly police interventions just don't happen anymore. Instead, she had effectively flagged up a drugs offence to the police, so now they had a process that would be followed, and it would have to run its course like any other criminal proceeding. A tough lesson for both mother and son.

AFTERWORD

Fuelled by Hope

When JfKL was first set up by Shauneen and I, there was no vehicle through which you could be a criminal lawyer in a charity. Legal aid contracts for criminal cases weren't available to charities, so to practise criminal law, we needed to be employed by a firm that had a legal aid contract. So we ended up setting up the charity as a community interest company and began employing staff and advocates through that for everything aside from the criminal law side, but we both remained employed by a law firm so that we could practise that bit as lawyers through the firm.

On the JfKL side of things, we were soon able to get contracts with the legal aid agency for areas such as community care law, which allowed lawyers to litigate against social services under the JfKL umbrella. While it wasn't ideal to be working in these two separate ways, it meant that apart from the criminal justice aspect, we could get funding for our JfKL objectives, and start building a base for our work.

Another law firm gave us office space in south London so we could expand our reach, and then we moved to another legal firm where they gave us a JfKL office in the basement with Shauneen now working there full time; employed me as lawyer upstairs; and offered their support. Theoretically, I was a lawyer three days a week for the firm, and two days a week I was running JfKL, but I ended up feeling like I had to fit in five days a week for each of them, as they were both such busy and crucial sets of work.

We will always be grateful to the law firms that supported us in those early days, as without them JfKL would have had a much tougher time getting up and running. But there were disadvantages to the set-up, too. There were always going to be those tensions that arise out of the different objectives of a charity versus a profit-making organization. In one of the profit-making firms I was supposed to be undertaking all these billable hours as a lawyer and meeting a financial target, but I wouldn't be thinking about the fixed fee, I would be doing the absolute most that was needed for whichever child was my client at the time. It meant every week across the staff charts my name would be at the bottom in red, as I was bringing in the least money, even though I was doing as much, if not more than others in terms of hours. Thinking about the profit margin of a case just didn't sit well with me. I absolutely understand that a legal firm is a business, but when it comes to children, I just couldn't do anything other than give it my all – even if it meant going well beyond the hours that made financial sense. So even while we embedded ourselves in firms, the goal was always to find a way for JfKL to move on and allow our ethos to entirely encompass our work.

This need to bridge two organizations dominated our first twelve years – it was 2017 before what were called 'alternative business models and charities' were allowed to tender for a criminal aid contract. We pounced on that, and finally JfKL became standalone. We now have offices in Islington in north London and, up until recently, we had around forty staff, and helped around seventy children a year. It took a long time to make that dream a reality. However, sadly, due to a lack of funding, we have had to significantly reduce the size of our service again.

In the charity sector the constant struggle for funding can be a huge drain on time, morale and emotions, and in the recent financial climate, it has proven to be even trickier. It broke my heart to reduce the number of projects we were able to keep working on within JfKL. But we have managed to hold on to the work at our core, focusing on the areas where children and young people most frequently have their rights breached, and where power is abused in the criminal justice system.

In many ways I wish I didn't have to write this book. I wish that we had a legal system that focused on safeguarding young people and helping them onto the right path, and that it was all transparent and open, and parents understood everything that was required of them and their children. But unfortunately, we are very far from that!

However, as the general public becomes more aware of just what a mess the youth criminal justice system seems to be in, they are rightfully starting to ask questions about it and how it can be improved. As part of that, I have found that my role has sometimes been called into question – by working in such a broken system, am I actually complicit with it? Does basing my career within a set-up that is so woeful, signal some kind of support and approval? It would be easy to become defensive at this kind of criticism, but I can actually understand the thought process, and it is good for me to stand back and look at the big picture from time to time, and debate the best way forward.

Ultimately, I see it that while we have children held in custody, or being taken through the courts, you have to have people working within the system, in all sorts of roles, to try to improve it. This is the system that exists here and now, whether we like it or not, so we need people who are looking to make the experience at the police station less scary, allowing a child's voice to be heard, or trying to get the right outcome for a case. That is still really important, both for those individual young people for whom that moment could be life-changing, and also in ensuring someone is holding the system to account internally on a daily basis.

Just for Kids Law is not alone in thinking like this either. There is a small but growing number of youth workers, lawyers and judges who are going above and beyond what is required of them and doing all they can to help make the youth criminal justice system a more functional, fair space for those within it, with the safeguarding of children at its heart.

I was on the judging panel for the Legal Aid Lawyer of the Year awards in 2023, and reading the details of the amazing lawyers who had been nominated, particularly in the 'Newcomer' category, really blew me away. They are all doing incredible things, really trying to achieve change by using the tool of the law, but also getting involved in community engagement, organizing, campaigning, setting up their own not-for-profits … the creativity, passion and commitment is phenomenal to see. It leaves me feeling that the future of legal aid is in good hands.

But equally, there is perhaps a limit to what we can do and say from within, as we still have to respect certain boundaries and laws, so I definitely think there is a place for other ways of making changes. People who are campaigning from the outside looking in, whether that is by looking at the bigger picture and advocating for change that way, or focusing on one singular change to the youth justice system and unapologetically tackling that, all add up to a possibility for real change. Putting all these methods of working together, functioning collaboratively, is the best way we are going to achieve the system our young people deserve.

In early 2023 the government seemed to be intent on diminishing civil liberties in this country, whether by clamping down on the right to protest, or changing immigration laws, and it feels as though there is a rising tension about our country's future. Thankfully, that kind of developing tension can lead to great things when funnelled in the right way, and seeing people pushing back gives me a growing reason for hope among the negativity. Emerging pockets of community activism mean that people are campaigning at grassroot levels, on everything from racism to issues with the police, to achieve positive outcomes for children and young people. They are making use of reports such as the Casey review of 2023, an independent investigation into the Metropolitan Police. Commissioned after the murder of Sarah Everard by Wayne Couzens, a serving officer, the Review highlighted toxic behaviour and numerous failings in the force, and was pretty damning about its sexism, racism and homophobia. The review also noted that the Met had made changes to priorities which left workforces such as those on child protection overworked and underfunded, putting children at a greater risk.

The review has armed campaigners with a tool that enables them to hold the Met Police to account. People are able to express their outrage and make clear that the system isn't good enough and they aren't going to stand for it. One example of members of the public grouping together in this way would be the case of Chris Kaba, an unarmed young man shot and killed by a police officer in south London. His family and the local community have led a campaign to get to the bottom of what happened and hold someone accountable, to ensure

Chris's killing wasn't just swept under the carpet. While it was a horrendous incident, responses like this give me hope that we are on the right road to improvement. I am always hopeful – you have to be fuelled by hope to work in this sector.

And then of course there are the young people themselves. They might struggle to stay on the right path at times, or make bad decisions, but given the right support, I really, truly have faith in our young people, and am keen to encourage them to feel the same. When given a sense of confidence, this activism for change can actually be driven by young people themselves. I look at the young campaigners now based at Coram Children's Legal Centre, where JfKL has transferred some of our projects, as an example of this. I see these young people who had been excluded from school, were homeless or caught up in the criminal justice system, now getting their message out there, fighting for change, speaking in Parliament. I feel overwhelmed with hope that it will be in their hands, as well as ours, to make changes that will see a brighter future filled with possibilities for all our children and young people.

If enough people take responsibility, step up and push for change, it will happen.

Acknowledgements

The first person I need to thank is Shauneen, without whom there would be no JfKL. We realized we were kindred spirits from the moment we began speaking and were soon to become the best of friends, too. Shauneen, you push and inspire me, and are the perfect partner in crime – literally!

Then there are all the staff who have brought the idea of JfKL to life over the last eighteen years. It is not a nine-to-five job and we've all grown and supported each other along the way. Thank you to my current legal team, Karolina, Robbie, Aisha, Amour, Jeremy and Judy as well as the other staff, Julie, Alan, Lorna and Mandeer, who put their heart and soul into JfKL every day, in particular Louise King, who runs JfKL with me today.

Thanks too to the committed and compassionate barristers who work alongside us – you are always showing me how to be a better lawyer. Special thanks to Danielle Manson, Susan Wright, Stella Harris, Anya Lewis, Brenda Campbell and Daniel Jameson, Cassan Lindsay and Justin Johnson, Jo Cecil and Garden Court Chambers.

Thank you to the JfKL trustees, who give their time and energy, a special thank you to Anthony Landes (Chair 2022–23) and the funders who have kept us afloat at the trickiest of times. You know who you are and are appreciated.

I can't forget those who gave Shauneen and me their support in the early days – Lawrence Lederman of Lawrence and Co., who allowed us to take the first step and run a CIC from his firm while practising as solicitors; Hemini Patel and Fadi Daoud who made me the lawyer I am today; Greg Stewart of G.T. Stewart, who allowed us to establish our south

London base; Patrick Allan of Hodge Jones & Allen where we created our North London base, spearheaded by Sandra Paul.

Thanks also go to Melanie Stooks, who inspired me when I was a Youth Justice Officer, and others who have never stopped lending their support – Ruth Haman, Katya Moran, Maya Sikand, Laura Janes and Fiona Bawdon. Others who were integral at our inception, Max Alexander and Carolyn Regan, and others who worked with us and continued their supported along the way, Kate Aubrey Johnson, Laura Cooper and Jennifer Twite.

The idea for this book came from a conversation between Lesley O'Mara and Enver Solomon. Thank you both for seeing the potential, as well as to Louisa McGeehan who championed and read the book in its infancy. Thanks to Emma Donnan, your perseverance in writing this with me has been phenomenal, as well as your ability to capture my views, feelings and passion; and to my editor at Michael O'Mara, Louise Dixon – your patience has known no bounds, and for that I am ever thankful! To everyone else who has given their advice, expertise and input to this book, thank you.

My job is a part of me, so my family have had no choice but to live and breathe JfKL too: thank you for doing so with love and understanding. My partner Randolph (I'm so sorry I didn't choose corporate law …) and my children, Jacob and Isaac, alongside Shauneen's family, have literally walked the walk with us. I remember bouncing Shauneen's new-born, Frankie, on my knee when going through our caseload in the early days.

To my mum and dad – in many ways you grew, learned and developed stability along with us. Your values, desire to challenge the system, and rebellious streaks really shaped my path, and the emotional and financial support from yourselves and my stepfather, Pete, has been immense. I also can't thank you enough for the support and love you provide as grandparents, alongside my parents-in-law, which allowed me to commit to this work and JfKL in the way that I have.

Thank you to all my siblings who created the rich tapestry of our childhood, in particular my sister Bianca who was there through it all. And to my extended family – grandmother, aunts, uncles and cousins – and the friends who have supported me and kept me sane, thank you.

Finally, to all the children in the legal system, past or present, who have placed their trust in us, thank you, this book is for you.

Contacts

You will find more specific sources of help at the end of each chapter.

TO CONTACT JUST FOR KIDS LAW

Have a look at our website www.justforkidslaw.org for more info on JfKL, news on our latest campaigns, and ways you can get involved. There is information there on how to get in touch if you are looking for help or advice on any of the areas we cover.

We also have an emergency twenty-four-hour Crime Contact Line, for anyone arrested out of office hours and needing immediate legal advice. Details of this number are on the website.

WHERE ELSE TO FIND HELP

- **Local Authority Contacts:** If you are under eighteen and you feel unsafe, or you are worried about someone who is under eighteen, you should contact the relevant local authority duty/out of hours service. These are open twenty-four hours a day, seven days a week. To find the duty number, Google your borough and then look for the children's services duty number (e.g. *'Brent children's services duty number'*).

- **NSPCC:** Well known for their work to prevent the abuse of children, their helpline (0808 800 5000) is there for any child concerned about their own safety, or any adult wanting to report concerns about a child. www.nspcc.org

Index

A

Abianda 144
Accessories and Abettors Act (1861)
    108
Action Against Public Authorities
    (AAPA) 186
Adedeji, Ademola 116
ADHD (attention deficit
    hyperactivity disorder) 88–9,
    155, 158, 161
adult, defined 21, 209–15
adultification bias 86, 191–8
adversarial system 225–6
adverse childhood experiences
    (ACEs) 130
age of criminal responsibility 67–9
Amendment 32 campaign 214–15
American Automobile Association
    Foundation (AAAF) 102
anti-terrorism 31
appropriate adult, defined 21
arrest:
    conditions/situations that increase
        chance of 17–18
    long-term effect of 25, 124
    reasonable force and right to
        silence 187
Art Not Evidence campaign 115
assault, degrees of 146–7
Asset/AssetPlus scoring tool 189–91
autism 88, 155, 156–8, 161–5, 169,
    173, 173–6, 249, 251–2
Avon and Somerset Police 83

B

BAME 18, 83, 177–208
barristers, described 220–2
Become (charity) 154
behaviour policies 78, 148
behavioural issues, instigating
    factors 15, 158, 173
Belamouadden, Sofyen 103–5
Bhatt Murphy Solicitors 208
Bindmans 208
Black Box Research 139
Black Lives Matter (BLM) 179, 184
Blakemore, Sarah-Jane 99, 106
    pack mentality 100–2
body language 157, 162
Body Worn footage 163, 183–4, 187,
    195, 207
brain development 97–100, 109, 211
Brecani ruling 138, 139

C

care system 11, 17, 46, 109, 134,
    145–54
case law 48, 109
Caseworks 246
Casey Review (2023) 259
CCTV evidence 20, 36, 64–7
Central Criminal Court of England
    and Wales (Old Bailey) 103,
    219, 226–8
Chair of the Bench 78
Channel 4 116
Charing Cross Police Station 104
charity sector, funding 257
Chartered Legal Executives 202
child, defined 209–15
child abuse 126, 128, 145
Child and Adolescent Mental
    Health Services (CAMHS) 156
Child Q 86–7
child spies 214–15
children in cells 38–40

Children's Act (1989) 152
Children's Commissioner for
    England 86
children's homes 39, 134–5, 142,
    145–54, 191, 248
  behaviour policies 148
  systemic failure 149–54
Children's Society 130, 144
chronic fatigue 172
City and Hackney Safeguarding
    Children Partnership (CHSCP)
    86
civil action 184, 204
classism 203
client confidentiality 49
common law 68
contempt of court 58, 165
contextual safeguarding 141, 190
Coram Children's Legal Centre 90,
    260
Coram Voice 154
costs (financial), of legal
    representation 234–41
counselling 74, 86, 105, 164, 176,
    245–6
county drug lines 127–44
court appearances 45–70
Court of Appeal 138, 206, 215
Couzens, Wayne 258
Covert Human Intelligence Sources
    (Criminal Conduct) Bill 214–15
covert intelligence 214–15
Covid-19 50, 51, 54, 75, 88, 155,
    169, 179, 247
CPS, see Crown Prosecution Service
Crown Court 47, 51, 76, 77, 199–
    200, 204, 217–41
  adjustments for children 223–4
  barristers 220–2
  judge and jury 218–20
  Old Bailey 103, 219, 226–8
Crown Prosecution Service (CPS)
    31–2, 36, 42, 55, 60, 62, 96, 98,
    107, 135, 137, 139, 141, 179,
    184, 214, 218, 223, 230–1, 235,
    240
  described 63–7
  ten-point checklist 148–9

D

Davis, Jahnine 192
DBS checks 150–1, 244
'Decriminalize the Classroom: A
    Community Response to Police
    in Greater Manchester's Schools'
    (NPMP) 83
defunding movement 43
depression 136, 172, 176
developmental disorders 158, 163
digital footprint 112, 113
disabilities 83, 88–9, 106, 136
disclosure 19–20, 23, 25, 29, 65–6,
    66, 77, 104, 244
Disclosure and Barring Service
    (DBS) 150, 244
disruptive behaviour 88, 89, 91, 132,
    136, 168
district judge (DJ) 53, 56
doli incapax 68
drug dealing 23, 61, 86, 127–44
  Home Office 2017 report 130
duty solicitor, defined 48–9

E

Eastman, Dr Oliver 122
ECHR (European Convention on
    Human Rights) 212
Elizabeth II 222
ethnic minorities 18, 83, 177–208
ethnicity 19, 83, 177–9, 199, 202
Everard, Sarah 259
exclusion, *see* school exclusion
exploitation 15, 23, 91, 127–44, 157,
    166, 219, 237–8

F

Family Action 154
fatalism 211
Feltham Prison and Young Offender
    Institution (YOI) 12–14, 15
Firmin, Carlene 141
first responder, defined 137
Floyd, George 179
football hooliganism 114
foresight 97–100, 103, 105–6, 114,
    164, 175, 211
foster care 152
free school meals 81
freedom of information (FOI) 184
friendship 95–110

G

grievous bodily harm (GBH) 58–9
grooming 129, 131–4, 138–9, 142–
    3, 144, 164
Guantanamo Bay 31
guilty by association 95–8, 105–10,
    117, 175, 201, 223

H

harmful sexual behaviour 122–3
Hodge Jones & Allen Solicitors
    (HJA) 208
Home Office:
    child spies 214–15
    Code of Practice 215
    Concordat on Children in
        Custody (2017) 38–40, 130
    modern slavery statistical bulletin
        137–8
homelessness 15, 241, 260
homophobia 259
House of Commons Justice
    Committee 105
Howard League for Penal Reform
    202

I

'incapable of deceit' (*doli incapax*)
    68
Independent Office for Police
    Conduct (IOPC) 185–7, 204
Independent Police Complaints
    Commission (IPCC) 186
Independent Review Panel (IRP)
    90–1
informal conversation 33–4
inquisitorial system 225
Islamophobia 178

J

Janes, Dr Laura 202
JENGbA (Joint Enterprise Not
    Guilty by Association) 106, 110
Johnson, Kim 108
joint enterprise 95–8, 105–10, 117,
    175, 201, 223
    defined 96–7
Joint Enterprise (Significant
    Contribution) Bill 108
Joseph-Salisbury, Dr Remy 82–3
judge and jury, described 218–20
judges, and racism 199–201
judicial review 210, 211, 212
Just for Kids Law (JfKL):
    created 16
    Crime Contact Line 262
    education 11–12
    funding 90, 169, 215, 241, 255–7
JUSTICE 115, 215

K

Kaba, Chris 184–5, 259–60
Khan, Sadiq 130
Kids of Colour project 83
King's Counsel (KC) 222, 228
knife crime 71–4, 97–8, 105–6

L

lack of foresight 103, 114, 211
Lambe, Shauneen 16, 210, 212, 255
Lammy Review (2017) 178–9, 200,
    202, 204, 206
language/speech difficulties 17
Leatherbrow, Kesia 213–14
Leaving Care guidelines 109
Legal Aid Agency 159, 186–7, 255
Legal Aid Lawyer of the Year 258
legal privilege 23, 236
Liberty Investigates 184
Lucy Faithfull Foundation 126

M

McKinnon, Gary 157
magic circle firm, defined 12
magistrates' court 15, 36, 45, 47, 51,
    54, 59, 199, 234, 240
mandatory sentencing 248
mental age 68, 109
mental health 17, 88–9, 111, 122,
    131, 136, 155–76, 192, 233, 251
mental maturity 109
Metropolitan Police ('Met') 40, 83,
    184, 186, 259
misconceptions 20, 34
mitigation 45, 49, 56–8, 203, 252
The Mix 176
Modern Slavery Act (2015) 136
Morgan, Rob 78
murder 22, 54–5, 103–7, 116,
    170–5, 179–80, 222–4, 227–32,
    239, 247–8

N

National Referral Mechanism
    (NRM) 136–8
neighbourhood policing 253–4
neurodiversity 89, 155, 161–6, 167
No Child In Cells campaign 38
'No comment' code 29, 121–2

No Police in Schools campaign 83
Notting Hill Carnival 184
NSPCC 122, 126, 262–3

O

obstruction 19–20, 20, 25–6, 43, 162
Oderinde, Abayomi 116
Old Bailey 103, 219, 226–8
online bullying 112–13
out-of-court disposal 35, 74, 108,
    243–4, 250–1
over-policing 78, 83, 180–5

P

pack mentality 97, 100–2
Paddington Green Police Station
    29, 31
Papyrus (charity) 176
pastoral care 87
pathological demand avoidance
    (PDA) 165
peer group pressure 97
peer pressure 15, 97, 101–3, 124,
    164, 250, 252
Police and Criminal Evidence Act
    (PACE) (1984) 85, 86
police conduct 42–3, 185–7
police custody guidelines 38–40
police interview 26–33
policing in school 80–5
poverty 15, 18, 130–1, 203
Power the Fight 144
pre-trial preparation 48
presumption in law 68
proactive defence 66
'problematic' behaviour 168
psychological assessments in school
    168
psychosis 155, 169–71, 171–6
PTSD (post-traumatic stress
    disorder) 139, 155, 166–7

public confidence statistical data, in
  the police 41–2
pupil referral unit (PRU) 91

Q
Queen's Counsel (QC) 222

R
racism 41, 86, 115, 177–208, 249,
  259
reasonable excuse 72–3, 78
reasonable force 34, 187
referral order (RO) 166, 244, 251
remorse 56, 165–6
representation, importance of
  199–203
restorative justice 245
right to silence 187
risk of exclusion, *see* school
  exclusion
Robinson, Dr Grace 139
Runnymede Trust 81, 83

S
safeguarding 22, 23, 71, 86–7, 137,
  141, 192, 214–15, 256–7
Safer London 144
Safer Schools Officer (SSO) 76–7, 83
St Giles Trust 144
Salvation Army 137
Samaritans 176
school-based police 80–5
school exclusion 18, 87–93, 125,
  131, 134, 160, 168–9, 173, 203
School Exclusions project 90
school playground disputes 6, 30,
  31, 80, 113–15, 162
school psychological assessments
  168
Secure Children's Home (SCH) 248

Secure Training Centre (STC) 248
self-defence 34, 75
self-harm 71–2, 143
SEND (Special Educational Needs
  and Disabilities) 88–90
Sense About Sexting campaign 120
sentencing:
  custodial placements 248–9
  disposal 35, 74, 108, 243–4, 250–1
  fair, definition of 249–52
  on licence 247–8
  mandatory 248
  options 243–59
  racism affects 204–6
  Referral Orders 166, 244, 251
  youth rehabilitation order (YRO)
    245
Sentencing Council 248
seventeen-year-olds in custody,
  rights of 209–15
sex and sexual relations 112
sex offenders register 123
sex, sexuality and sexual relations
  117–26, 128
sexism 198–9, 258
sexual exploitation 15, 23, 126, 133,
  137–42
sexual offences 47, 121–6, 167
sexual touching 193
shoplifting 47, 235, 239
single-parent homes 190
slavery 130, 136–40, 192, 194, 219
social communication issues 88, 163
  (*see also* autism)
social media 111–26
  addiction to 111–12, 120
  fake profiles 114
  sex and sexual relations 117–23
Social Services 21, 68, 109, 137–42,
  152, 167, 192, 195, 255
Soyoye, John 115
special needs 83, 88–9, 106, 131,
  161, 162–4, 168

speech/language difficulties 17
spent convictions 244
Statement of Special Educational
    Needs 89, 168
stop and search powers 177–8,
    181–3, 185, 206–8
StopWatch 208
substance abuse 15
suicide 176, 210–11, 213
Supreme Court 105, 106
surrogate family 148, 150, 151
systemic racism 115

T
teenage witnesses 229–34
terrorism 31, 178
trauma 12, 38, 40, 49, 53, 86, 104,
    115–16, 139, 148, 150, 155,
    166–7, 169, 195, 232–3
Truth and Lies Discussion (TLD)
    test 163, 229–30
TV crime dramas 46, 128, 199

U
UK Protected Persons Service
    (UKPPS) 231
unconscious bias 188–91, 193
UNCRC 68–9
underage sexual conduct 119, 124–6
undiagnosed health issues 88–9,
    131, 156–7, 159–61
Unjust (NFP organization) 208
Untold 116
'Urban Street Gangs, Child
    Criminal Exploitation and
    County Lines' (Robinson) 139

V
victim statements 17
vulnerability 6, 12–14, 16, 21, 86,

    111, 130, 134, 144, 151–2, 159,
    164, 169–70, 191–5, 213–14, 250

W
'what if?' situations 163
Wilson, Alexandra: *In Black and
    White* 196
witness protection 231
witness statements 20, 66, 85, 107,
    229–34

Y
YouGov 41
Young Offender Institution (YOI)
    248
youth court:
    Crown Court deferred to 217
    defence lawyer 57–60
    layout 51–2
    magistrates 52–6
    pre-trial preparation 48–51
    prosecution lawyer 60–2
youth courts 45–70
    defined 47
Youth Justice Board (YJB) 78, 248
Youth Justice Legal Centre 164
Youth Offending Teams (YOTs):
    client confidentiality 238
    described 15–16
    meeting formats 245–6
    YJB liaison 248
youth rehabilitation order (YRO)
    245